PREDATOR DEATHMATCH

NICK MOLLOY
WITH ILLUSTRATIONS BY ANTHONY WALLIS

Typeset by Jonathan Downes,
Edited by Clare-Elizabeth Clancy
Technical editor Max Blake
Illustrations © Ant Wallace 2009
(All my love to Aimee and peanut.
and to Mum, Dad and Shell - look, my name's on the cover!)
Cover and Layout by SPiderKaT for CFZ Communications
Using Microsoft Word 2000, Microsoft , Publisher 2003, Adobe Photoshop CS.

First published in Great Britain by CFZ Press

**CFZ Press
Myrtle Cottage
Woolsery
Bideford
North Devon
EX39 5QR**

© CFZ MMIX

All rights reserved. Without limiting the rights under copyright reserved above, no part of this publication may be reproduced, stored in or introduced into a retrieval system, or transmitted, in any form of by any means (electronic, mechanical, photocopying, recording or otherwise), without the prior written permission of both the copyright owners and the publishers of this book.

ISBN: 978-1-905723-45-4

Dedicated to Sexecute because without him I would never have had the time to write it

Also by the same author -

ROADWARRIOR : Confessions of a Male Stripper.
Pen Press (14 Feb 2009)

Contents

Page 7   Foreword by Dr Karl Shuker
Page 9   Introduction
Page 11 Chapter 1 – **Battle for the Seas**
             Great White Shark vs. Killer Whale
Page 27 Chapter 2 – **Battle for the Land**
             Polar Bear vs. Siberian Tiger
Page 43 Chapter 3 – **Terrestrial Battle of the Ages**
             Dinosaur King vs. Super croc
Page 65 Chapter 4 – **Aquatic Battle of the Ages**
             Megalodon vs. Megapli
Page 83 Chapter 5 – **Deep in the Ocean**
             Sperm Whale vs. Giant Squid
Page 97 Chapter 6 – **Living "Dinosaurs"**
             Komodo Dragon vs. Anaconda
Page 111 Chapter 7 – **Miscellaneous Predators**
Page 131 Conclusive Summary

Foreword

Every so often - but nowhere near often enough! - a book is published whose premise is so entertaining and thoroughly original that it seems incredible no-one has thought of writing just such a book long ago. *Predator Deathmatch* fits this description perfectly. The basic idea is simplicity itself - who would win a battle between two seriously major predators?

Each chapter pairs contenders from various ecosystems and time periods, setting up 'fight to the kill' matches between the polar bear and Siberian tiger, prehistory's monstrous giant shark Megalodon and a comparably formidable marine reptile of pliosaurian persuasion, the sperm whale and the giant squid, and so forth. Nick's vivid accounts of how he would expect these titanic slugfests to shape out make exciting reading, but what enhances his coverage immeasurably is the painstaking degree of factual research and provision of background pre- and post-fight information that he also provides. Moreover, whereas a welter of facts and figures might in the wrong hands be off-putting and even counterproductive to retaining the reader's interest, thanks to Nick's deft, infectiously enthusiastic style of writing, laced throughout with scintillating flashes of dry humour, the very substantial body of data that he incorporates into each chapter actually serves to engage interest even further. The net result is a book that is near-impossible to put down once you have begun reading it – after initially planning to read just the first chapter to begin with, simply to gain a feel for its style and depth before reading further, I found myself reading the entire manuscript from cover to cover at a single sitting, and enjoying every page of it immensely.

So if you've ever wondered who would emerge victorious should a great white shark and a killer whale clash lethally in the high seas, or if *T. rex* and a primeval mega-croc experienced a truly fatal encounter, or if Komodo's veritable dragon should somehow find itself assailing an anaconda of Pythonesque proportions, prepare for all of your questions – and many others that you hadn't even got around to posing – to be answered within the pages of this superb book, where the gladiators of past and present, land and sea are only awaiting your private audience before commencing their deadly duels. After all, who needs boxing and wrestling, or even cage fighting, when the greatest and most bloodthirsty marauders ever to stride this planet – like the *bona fide* colossi that they are, were, and remain – are ready to perform at your personal behest? So take your seat ringside, and don't forget your popcorn!

Introduction

I guess people will always be interested in the question of 'Who's the Daddy?' that is, who's the hardest, the meanest and the nastiest. Every school in the land will have its Daddy; the so-called 'hardest' pupil or *perceived* hardest pupil. When I was growing up, Big Daddy was the Daddy of wrestlers; the good guy character that was always just too much of a Daddy for all the bad guys.

Everywhere we turn in society people and their performances are ranked against each other: who earns the most, who's the strongest, who's got the biggest arms, who runs the fastest and ultimately who's the baddest man on the planet? Boxing's world heavyweight title has long been the most coveted prize in sport, consistently being representative of the sporting world's biggest revenue earner over the last forty years or so. The heavyweight boxers have never been the most entertaining in the fight game. That title is surely contested somewhere between the welterweights and the middleweights, who pack speed as well as power in their armoury. However, as they say, a good big 'un will always beat a good little 'un. Thus, by virtue of their size, the heavyweight titlists dispute the question of who is the ultimate Daddy. Although the dedicated pugilistic fan clambers to see the likes of Roy Jones, Bernard Hopkins and Floyd Mayweather before all others, the mass public demand to see the likes of the self-styled bad man, Mike Tyson. After all, in a street fight in his heyday he would surely have had few rivals.

Humans are somewhat unique amongst the animal kingdom in that throughout their society there is a recognised class system. Many people are born into privileges that are not afforded to others, thereby allowing them to opt out of 'the survival of the fittest'. They do not have to compete for jobs and the security that a steady income can bring. They do not have to worry about the day to day struggle to provide the needs of a basic existence. Many inherit jobs, wealth and security by nature of their birth.

In the animal kingdom (and certain levels of human societies) these luxuries are simply not afforded to their inhabitants. The rules of survival dictate that you must kill or be killed. In any given ecosystem there is a recognised hierarchy of predators and prey. One creature inevitably preys on another and in turn that creature is preyed upon by something else. This formula continues until we reach the 'apex predator' in a given environment. The apex predator has no natural enemies except, perhaps, others of its own species.

Man typically represents the apex predator in all environments because of his larger brain. He has developed technologies that can defeat even the most ferocious of predators. Even a *Tyrannosaurus rex* would be nothing in the face of man's technological weaponry. However, if we strip man of his weaponry, he is a puny excuse for a predator. Indeed, frequently man becomes the prey.

Popular films often demonstrate man as the prey of nightmarish nature. The 1975 movie *Jaws* could perhaps be blamed for starting the trend. Since then we have had shoals of piranhas, killer crocodiles, grizzly bears and over-sized snakes – to name but a few – terrorising and eating people in the name of entertainment. There is something about these creatures that draws us to them: a morbid fascination with things that can not only overpower and kill us, but then dine on us as well.

My morbid curiosity goes much further than that. I have often wondered who or what is the ultimate Daddy. Many creatures out there are capable of eating us, but I have often wondered which one of them is capable of eating the other. How big do they get? What would happen if we took one apex predator out of its natural environment and placed it in the environment of another apex predator? A North American grizzly bear will never meet a Sumatran tiger in the wild but assuming they did meet one day, and assuming that they were both starving, who would eat who?

This book attempts to answer these questions, questions that have long fascinated me and so it appears long fascinated everyone I talk to on the subject. Several fantasy match-ups have been mooted. Each chapter will delve into the backgrounds of the antagonists; their strengths, their weaknesses; and attempt to forecast the most likely outcome should they ever meet to decide who would win the ultimate predator shoot-out.

Chapter 1
Battle for the Seas

Great White Shark vs. Killer Whale

JAWS

Like many other people, my fascination with the great white shark sprang from watching the classic film *Jaws*. When *Jaws* first came out at the cinema I was only a year old. I have a vague recollection of being taken to the cinema to see *Jaws 2* when I was about four. I think I slept through most of it. However, when Jaws was shown on television for the first time it had my full attention.

Being only seven years of age I was still a little squeamish about watching people being eaten. Funnily enough, watching the little kid get eaten along with his airbed didn't bother me all that much. At the time he could have been me; he even had my haircut. But watching Quint the shark fisherman being eaten whole at the end was just too much for my infant stomach to take. I remember turning to look at my Dad while Quint was being chomped, a wry smile gradually rising on his face. It wasn't until the third time that I actually watched *Jaws* that I could watch it all the way through without turning my head (I was nine by then).

Being male I have long been fascinated by size and how big things get. With each subsequent *Jaws* movie the shark just got bigger and bigger. In the original movie Hooper the oceanographer, on seeing Jaws for the first time, states "that's a twenty-footer". He is immediately rebuffed by Quint: "Twenty-five [feet]; three tonnes of him". The original Jaws was a male shark, which in the real world, are smaller than their mates. When *Jaws 2* came along, the killer shark was female and measured a hefty 30 feet. Similarly, *Jaws 3* had increased by a further five feet. *Jaws 4* was so silly I have not dared to watch it again yet I seem to remember that the great white nemesis had increased again by five feet, giving us a whopping great white shark of 40 feet in length.

But, I hear you ask, how valid are these figures? Well, for many years accessing the sources available to me then, I believed these figures were well within the bounds of possibility, making the great white the undisputed Daddy of today's oceans. My very first *Guinness Book of Records* was the 1984 edition and I hurriedly devoured the section on animals. It stated that the biggest measured great white exceeded twenty-nine feet in length and had a girth of over twenty-one feet. It had been caught after a fierce battle with Azorean fishermen. However, an even larger female had been trapped in a net off the Californian coast in 1930 and this was said to exceed 37 feet in length.

Additionally, the same Christmas that I received my *Guinness Book of Records* I was given a large coffee-table-sized book on creatures of the world's oceans. It had its obligatory section on the white shark, which said 'It is the most dangerous shark to man because of its size – up to 12 metres (40ft) long. The great white has been responsible for frequent unprovoked attacks on both boats and swimmers'.

Also, I remember on two separate occasions my dad saying to me, on the basis of newspaper reports, that a shark 'as big as Jaws' had attacked and eaten surfers. No doubt their size had been estimated on the basis of bite marks made on surfboards, but I realise now that the 'as big as Jaws' tag was nothing more than tabloid hype.

When I was about thirteen I remember looking at a friend's *Guinness Book of Records* from around 1979. The first section I turned to was the 'Largest Shark' section. I was amazed to note that according to this earlier edition the largest white shark on record was a 43-footer; bigger than it was in my later edition.

In weighing up the viability of the white shark as the Daddy of the oceans, let us make it clear at this stage that if they did grow to 40+ feet there would be no rival for their title. The killer whale would likely succumb, and quickly. Megalodon, an ancient but now extinct relative of the great white, did not grow much beyond the 50-foot mark and it is known that Megalodon *did* dine heartily on whales. More on Megalodon later….

The movie *Jaws* and its resultant spin-offs appear to have played a major part in creating several mystiques about the great white shark. The first of those is certainly related to size. We now know that the average adult white shark is actually in the region of fourteen to fifteen feet in length. However, bigger specimens do of course occur.

Richard Ellis and John E. McCosker provide us with an excellent chapter on the size of the great white shark in their eponymous book on the subject. With regards to the 37-footer from 1930, a 1987 study obtained a tooth from the very same shark and concluded that it actually came from a shark that was sixteen to seventeen feet in length, not much above average. Their investigation into the twenty-nine-footer caught in the Azores revealed it to be nothing more than hyperbole.

Much of the blame for the exaggeration of the great white's size can also be laid firmly at the door of fishermen. Claims of their gigantic catches abound in the literature but disintegrate under careful scrutiny. The number of very large white sharks said to have been caught or sighted is huge. However, most of these are simply imaginary or wild exaggerations. Bigelow and Schroeder recount the story of an Australian shark, reported in the local newspapers as a sixteen-footer, which when measured, was only eight feet and six inches.

I have read many old books and articles referring to 'small' sharks of under twenty feet in length. We now know that a twenty-foot white shark is far from small. The largest white sharks, when accurately and scientifically measured, range between nineteen and twenty-one feet. However, there are some possibly credible twenty-three-footers backed up by photographs, if not measuring tape, vying for the Daddy title.

There seems little reason to doubt that there are or have been white sharks in the twenty-five-foot range. A recent documentary on the Discovery channel included a South African shark biologist who stated that in his youth a white shark 'roamed' near the coast where he lived. It was known by the local fisherman as the "submarine". The biologist had sighted it himself and stated that he had never seen a white shark like it, estimating its size to be in the region of seven metres (twenty-three feet). It stands to reason that the biggest white shark ever is probably bigger than any caught or sighted by man. Yet claims of 40-foot white sharks simply do not hold water (no pun intended). For the purposes of this contest our Daddy-vying shark will be a twenty-five-foot, three tonne specimen.

Also, it seems *Jaws* created the myth of the great white shark as a cold-blooded killer, chomping through bathers purely for the hell of it. Nothing could be further from the truth. Indeed, the great white shark seems to have quite discerning tastes as several people have found to their benefit.

The white shark's prey ranges from small fish, to large fish (including other sharks), dolphins, seals and whales. Its main prey item of choice seems to be fat-rich, blubbery seals. They pose little threat in terms of injury and are highly nutritious. Discoveries of human flesh or bones in the stomachs of white sharks are exceedingly rare. However, white shark attacks on humans have occurred almost annually in California, parts of South Africa and Australia; yet of all the white shark attacks on humans usually only one in ten is fatal.

Clearly this is not a failing in the predatory behaviour of the whites but more a result of their 'attack philosophy'. If they wanted to eat surfers they would eat them. There is little a surfer could do to defend himself, even against a juvenile white shark. Moreover, the survival of many tale-tellers is down to two main theories. The first states that the shark has made an error; whilst swimming below, the shark spots the surfer on his board, the resulting outline appearing very seal-like in the weak light and poor visibility. A slight adjustment of the pectoral fins sends the shark hurtling up towards the surface taking a large bite of the 'seal'. Upon biting the human, instead of tasting rich, tasty, nutritious blubber, the shark tastes bony stringy flesh. Realising the error, the shark moves off in search of tastier prey, leaving the injured human to survive another day.

Although this may be a possibility, it would appear that white shark feeding strategy goes beyond this. It isn't only humans that survive the first bite. Many pinnipeds have been sighted ashore with injuries sustained as a result of white shark attacks. Indeed, it would appear that the white sharks bite then spit their prey. The massive first bite means that most of their prey weakens and bleeds to death before the shark again moves in to devour its quarry. This is a 'safety first' approach that ensures the shark receives minimum damage from the prey item.

The hunted prey can indeed be quite large. Dolphins have frequently been found in the stomachs of white sharks. Male elephant seals, which can weigh up to 4 tonnes, have been attacked, injured and eaten by whites. Whale bones as much as 10,000 years old have borne scratches that suggest white shark predation (although it is unclear if this is a result of scavenging). Furthermore, today's whites are known to feed on living whales, as watched by Theodore Walker, who saw four whites feeding on a young grey whale off California. Moreover, there is some emerging evidence from New Zealand researchers suggesting that white sharks may actually hunt whales as a family unit. One theory emanating from this research is that some whale beachings are the result of the whales fleeing predation from the white sharks.

Does the great white shark actually have anything to fear in today's oceans?

Predator Deathmatch

GREAT WHITE SHARK IN PROFILE

Length	15 feet average up to a maximum of 25 feet. (7.5 metres)
Weight	1.5 tonnes, up to a maximum of 3 tonnes
Weaponry	Over 100, 2-inch-long serrated teeth made for ripping and tearing.
Speed	Up to 20mph
Weaknesses	Not as big as once thought
Profile	Solitary predator, feeding mainly on small pinnipeds, but known to take dolphins, whales and elephant seals.
Human Champ	Evander Holyfield throws a good right hand but has it bitten off at the shoulder. He is bitten in half 13 seconds into the bout.

THE BLACK DEATH

The killer whale, or Orca, was given its common name by early whalers who saw them ripping chunks of flesh from harpooned whales. Marvelling at their strength and speed (up to 30mph), the Killer Whale was christened. Yet despite the frightening name, killer whales do not possess the same killer reputation in human folklore that is owned by the great white shark.

This may have something to do with the fact that killer whales can be seen playing with humans daily in places such as Seaworld, Florida. Far from eating people, the intelligence of the killer whale has allowed us to train them into oversized pets. Furthermore, films such as *Free Willy* have caused us to fall in love with these giants, turning the captive killer into a creature worthy of human pity. Also, perhaps surprisingly, there is no known instance of a wild orca killing a human. Popular culture therefore dictates that there is little to fear from the killer whale, instead seeing it as a sensitive, almost gentle creature. However, the truth is far removed from the popular perception. In an almost total role reversal of the white shark, the orca has a reputation that is considerably understated.

The killer whale is actually the largest of the dolphins. It inhabits all the world's oceans with the largest numbers in the colder seas near both poles. Generally preferring deep water, killer whales do enter bays, inland seas and estuaries. Termed broadly there are two types of killer whale: transients and residents.

Residents, a docile type, tend to live the whole year round in one particular area and largely eat fish. They are also relatively easy to study and follow. Far less is known about transients on the other hand. They roam far and wide and their diet consists of just about anything that takes their fancy. Indeed, it is the behaviour of the transients that earned the orcas the tag of 'wolves of the sea'.

Although both transients and residents belong to the same species, they behave very differently. They often share a territory, but do not mix, do not mate and do not even seem to notice each other. Indeed, it is thought that the two groups may not have interbred for hundreds, even thousands of generations. DNA samples have been extracted from both groups of killer whales and they have remained apart long enough to have begun diverging physically although it is thought that they have yet to diversify enough genetically to be incompatible. Thus far, it appears that only cultural differences keep the transients and residents from breeding.

Both sets of orcas live in large pods and are pack hunters. Residents live almost purely off fish, working cooperatively to round large shoals of fish together and then stunning then with devastating sweeps of their tails. This allows another member of their family group to take a big mouthful of the giddy fish.

Transients on the other hand are well deserving of the title 'killer'. The 'wolves of the sea' roam the oceans in search of mammalian prey. Transient killers consume huge numbers of marine mammals annually and their predatory habits are a significant force in shaping marine communities. For example, a whole ecosystem has been altered along a 600-mile stretch of the

Aleutian Islands because killer whales have begun consuming sea otters due to a decline in pinniped numbers. Due to a decline in sea otters, sea urchin numbers have exploded. In turn the sea urchins have ravaged the sea kelp, which used to provide habitat for fish, which in turn provided food for eagles and other fish otters. The impact on the ecosystem has been significant due to the changed dietary pattern of the killers.

However, transient killer whales hunting in packs have been known to take far bigger prey than pinnipeds or sea otters. Off the coasts of Antarctica, killers are well known for their practice of eating just the fleshy lips and tongue of Minke whales before leaving their victims to die. Their diets are extremely diverse. In his book on whales, Martin states "known to be taken in various parts of the world are at least twenty-four species of cetacean (whale), five species of pinniped (seal), the dugong, 30 species of fish, seven species of bird, two species of squid, in addition to a variety of other warm and cold blooded sea creatures such as turtles".

Indeed, even the blue whale, the largest creature in the ocean at over 100 feet long and 150 tonnes falls victim to a pack of transient killers. Such an incident has been famously caught on film. A pack of approximately 30 killer whales rip chunks out of the hapless blue whale until it bleeds to death.

The average adult male killer whale reaches a total body length in the region of twenty-three to twenty-four feet, although very large specimens can exceed 30 feet. The average weight of an adult male is in the region of five tonnes; very large specimens can approach ten tonnes. Females are smaller, averaging around twenty feet in length and weighing approximately three tonnes. The mouth of a killer whale is well equipped to deal with large prey, having ten to twelve pairs of large, oval-sectioned teeth in both upper and lower jaws.

Also, just when you thought it was safe on the beach, the killer whales come out of the water in search of their prey. Specific pods have been known to rush out of the surf onto steep beaches in an attempt to pluck seals from their 'safe havens'. Having beached themselves, they then wriggle their way back into the sea, a hapless seal trapped in their jaws. They then completely dispel any notion of the benign *Free Willy* image, as they begin tossing their hapless victim – still alive, though stunned – to each other in what can only be described as a sickening game of tennis. Why the killers participate in this 'sport' is unknown, but education of their young is a possibility.

Even sperm whales, the largest of the toothed whales, and arguably the largest predatory hunter to have ever lived, are not free from the wrath of the killers. Orca attacks on sperm whales have only been recorded a handful of times, but they *do* occur and again, this was caught on film in 1997.

A gang of nine adult female sperm whales had formed a rosette, their heads pointing towards the centre, their tails pointing outwards, acting as a defensive weapon. However, this method of defence did not prove effective against the pack of killers. Over a period of five hours, the killer whales repeatedly rushed the huddled sperm whales, submerging to attack from beneath just before they hit the huddle.

Eventually, one adult sperm whale was killed and devoured by the killers. Instead of targeting a specific individual the killers had attacked at random and had injured every member of the sperm whale herd. No injuries were visible on the killer whales. The scientists who witnessed this attack stated they had previously believed that sperm whales, due to their size, cooperative herding behaviour and deep diving proclivities were largely exempt from the pressures of killer whale predation. This is clearly not always the case.

The sperm whales in this case were adult females in the region of 30-35 feet as opposed to twenty feet for the killers. The scientists could not understand why the sperm whales, in this instance, did not attempt to defend themselves more aggressively. Old whaling accounts are filled with graphic descriptions of sperm whales lashing out and destroying longboats when under attack themselves.

Although smaller than males, these sperm whales considerably outweighed their attackers. Also, they can dive far deeper and for far longer periods than killer whales can. However, the killer whales can reach maximum speeds in the region of 30mph as opposed to 6mph for the sperm whales. Maybe the sperm whales felt they lacked the fins (legs) to get away.

Interestingly, about five days after this attack scientists again saw an encounter between killer and sperm whales. This time, when the sperm whales detected the killers they closed ranks into a group of about 50, lining up in a parallel line, all facing the same direction. Whether they did not feel so bold this time, or were just not as hungry, for some reason the killers did not attack.

Clearly, transient orcas in particular are very deserving of the label 'killer whale'. The forces that represent media marketing do not do the killer justice in the Daddy stakes. Shamu the cartoon killer whale might give you a nice smile, but his transient friends will smile as they eat you for breakfast with a blue whale steak.

Interestingly, in the wake of the *Jaws* phenomenon a film was released in 1977 titled *Orca*, in which a killer whale does actually attack and kill humans. However, as I seem to remember (I have only seen it once when I was about ten) this was because an old whaler attacked and killed the mate of the aggressive killer whale. Even in this poor *Jaws* imitation, you couldn't help but sympathise with the killer whale, simply avenging the murder of his mate.

However, the question remains does the killer whale have what it takes to tame Jaws?

Predator Deathmatch

KILLER WHALE IN PROFILE

Length	23-24 feet average, up to a maximum of 33 feet (10 metres)
Weight	5 tonnes average, maximum 10 tonnes
Weaponry	10-12 pairs of large, oval-sectioned, enamelled teeth in both upper and lower jaws
Speed	Up to 30mph
Weaknesses	Prettyboy Image
Profile	Pack hunter, known collectively as the 'wolves of the sea.' Feeds on mammalian prey of all sizes, including the blue whale.
Human Champ	Evander Holyfield opens cautiously, landing a nice jab on the nose of his opponent with no effect. A sudden burst of speed from the orca results in Holyfield being shaken violently in a death grip, before being thrown over twenty feet through the air, causing him

to land awkwardly. The orca circles Holyfield in confident anticipation before a devastating surge from below results in the orca severing a leg, causing an end to the carnage after 31 seconds of the bout.

BIG FIGHT PREVIEW

This is a very difficult one to call. The popular favourite is surely the great white shark; the marauding, all-consuming, ruthless, cold-blooded killer conjured from the recesses of our nightmares. Yet science has recently cut the great white down to size. No longer do gargantuan killer sharks of *Jaws* proportions roam the oceans. We now know that a twenty-foot white is like a man of six-foot-nine; they exist but are unusual.

The killer whale will have a considerable size and weight advantage going into this bout. Additionally, the killer will be more manoeuvrable and has a higher top speed. Yet the white shark is capable of tremendous turns of speed and it is unlikely that the killer whale will be able to gain an advantage from this area.

Interestingly, clashes between killer whales and white sharks are not completely unknown, either in fiction or fact. In *Jaws 2* a killer whale was washed up on the beach, a presumed victim of the killer shark. When asked whether a white shark could have done this, the expert replied that it was possible but it would have to be a very large shark (at 30 feet it certainly qualified as that). But what about in the real world?

In 1997 this particular clash of the titans was actually caught on tape when a killer whale attacked and killed a great white shark. Much was made of this attack as marine biologists had always assumed that these two apex predators had tended to avoid each other.

The video was shot by wildlife enthusiasts who had been alerted by a radio transmission from a fisherman who had spotted two orcas in the area. The expedition found the orcas – an adult female around twenty feet in length and her calf. Suddenly another dark shape appeared in the water giving the orcas a wide berth. The adult orca then veered towards the dark shape and surged to the surface with a ten-foot white shark in its jaws, which it began thrashing on the surface of the water. When it had killed the shark the adult orca encouraged her calf to feed.

This has been used in some quarters to argue that the killer whale is the undisputed Daddy of the seas. However, this evidence is not really admissible. The victim white shark was only a juvenile. As a white shark increases in size, particularly upwards of ten feet, its girth becomes disproportionate to its increase in length. That is, it becomes much heavier.

The teeth of young white sharks (ten feet or shorter) differ considerably from those of their parents. Juvenile whites have relatively long, narrow teeth for grasping slippery fish, whereas the teeth of adults become much broader at the base, enabling them to ambush and cut through much larger, tougher prey. As the white grows its agility declines and it becomes unable to catch fish and other mobile prey items. Accordingly, it is forced to mug and murder larger, slower prey.

An adult white shark would surely have had little difficulty in dispatching the killer whale calf in much the same way that the adult killer whale had little difficulty disposing of the juvenile white.

Interestingly, literature possibly alludes to previous clashes between orcas and whites. In *The Shark*, a 1970 book by Jacques-Yves and Philippe Cousteau, the authors repeat a story told to them by a Doctor Theodore Walker, a grey whale researcher. Walker claimed he witnessed an event whereby a group of killer whales were playing in the water off Baja, California while about half a mile away, a nine- or ten-foot shark was swimming lazily.

Suddenly one of the whales plunged vertically into the sea and disappeared, only to reappear about three minutes later, leaping clear of the water with the shark held crosswise in its mouth. The species of shark was not mentioned, but the account immediately followed a discussion of white sharks feeding on grey whale carcasses in the lagoons of Baja. Did the Cousteaus mean to imply that the shark was a white?

One might begin to conclude that the odds are stacked against Jaws in this clash of the marine giants. However, if the Walker-witnessed incident is another example of an orca killing a great white, it only serves to present another example of the 1997 incident. A nine- or ten-foot white shark is a juvenile, not an adult and therefore not a worthy opponent to an adult killer whale. Write off Jaws at your peril!

SECONDS OUT

The ocean's two most feared predators approach each other cautiously. Although a good seven feet longer than his opponent, at thirty three feet long the male killer whale keeps a healthy distance from the female white shark. That eerie, toothy grin commands respect, whoever you are. Similarly, she also keeps her distance, considerably outweighed by the black and white mass in front of her. Both are hungry, neither has eaten for some time, and just about now seems appropriate to lay the dinner table With the stalemate seeming everlasting the killer makes the first move. A few swishes of that hugely powerful tail propels him to nearly 30 miles per hour, rushing headlong towards the shark. Jaws, however, can also produce a tremendous turn of speed, narrowly causing the killer to miss as it speeds past her right flank. The incredibly powerful and damaging jaws of the white shark close as she attempts to take a sizeable chunk out of the passing orca. But the attempt is in vain. Both leviathans regroup. It is the killer who again takes the lead, first diving below the shark and then shooting up with tremendous power and speed. The shark is caught unawares and it takes evasive action too late, sustaining a powerful butt from the killer. Stunned though not wounded, the shark retreats slowly; but too slowly. The killer repeats its previous attack, with similar results.

The shark turns as if to flee, the killer begins a repeat of its previous success. Yet the shark does not flee; she turns quickly back towards her fast approaching tormentor. Surprised and perhaps unnerved by this manoeuvre, the killer alters its course. This presents the shark with a golden opportunity to sink its teeth into the rear of the passing killer. First blood belongs to the great white, but this was no killer blow to the orca. The great white was unable to get a good grip on its opponent and has only ripped a small piece from the killer's side.

The whale backs off, bleeding from the gash on its flank; the shark does likewise, its bite and spit instinct telling it to wait for its prey to bleed and die. But this is no seal. The killer may have *backed* off, but he has not *run* off. After regrouping he returns for more, this time diving deeper than before, then propelling himself at the shark. This time the killer scores a big hit, sinking his teeth into the side of the shark. The shark did not expect this sudden attack and has been caught unawares whilst waiting for the prey item to weaken. Far from weakening, the prey has just launched the best attack of the bout. The whale attempts to shake the shark but the shark is too big, swimming hastily away and bleeding heavily. The killer pursues and catches the shark, this time obtaining a grip on its tail. Again the killer thrashes its body from side to side but this time the shark retaliates, freeing its tail, turning and sinking its teeth into the flesh of the killer without obtaining a good grip. The killer is bleeding again; the shark is again fleeing. The killer instinctively pursues its quarry, this time butting into the shark without sinking its teeth. The shark continues to flee, bleeding far more profusely than the orca. This time the killer lets the shark swim freely away. He has sustained another injury himself and is wary of another. Anyway, next time he will have his other pod members with him and as a unit they will make a proper meal of the shark. He has seen off the great white but he did not conquer her.

Verdict: Killer whale crowned king of the ocean by points decision.

POST FIGHT ANALYSIS

In the light of the Orca's victory, some observers are now questioning the right of Jaws to call herself an apex predator. Such musings have been circling the scientific community for several years particularly in light of the 1997 incident where the juvenile white became lunch to an adult Orca. In recent years, further evidence has emerged to cement the position of the killer dolphin. That particular 1997 clash of our ocean daddies occurred off the Californian coast. There are numerous killer whale and white shark researchers studying behaviours in that part of the world. It was noted that after the incident occurred the white sharks disappeared. The 'flight of the whites' has been pointed to as evidence from the Orca camp that the whites are just big scaredy fish that run away at the first sight of trouble.

In the initial reports of the incident, it was claimed that the adult Orca appeared to be encouraging her calf to feed. However, on reviewing the footage, whale researchers have claimed that they know the individual responsible for the attack and claim that she does not have a calf, contradicting the initial reports. They raised the question of whether this is a straight act of normal predation. Killer whales are exceptionally intelligent hunters. They adapt their methods of attack towards their prey items dependent on the intended victim. In the case of some species of shark, there exists a state referred to as tonic immobility. When the shark is turned upside down, it can enter a state of paralysis. Scientists have exploited this phenomenon to study shark behaviour. Although not conclusive, anecdotally it appears that the Orca may have tried to invert the white shark deliberately to instil a state of tonic immobility and therefore reduce resistance and threat to the Orca. If this were the case, it would suggest that Orcas regularly predate on and hunt sharks. However, it does not mean that they regularly hunt and prey on *white* sharks.

Researchers trying to design the ultimate shark repellent have noted that certain sharks are particularly repelled by the scent of their own dead. Indeed, this scent is so potent that it can cause certain sharks to come out of a state of tonic immobility. It has been postulated that the 'flight of the whites' was caused because they were able to smell one of their own dead. In the year 2000, another event occurred off the Californian coast. Killer whales again turned up in white shark territory. Although no attack was witnessed, a commotion was seen out on the ocean by a researcher and he speculates that another white became an Orca lunch. In the case of a tagged adult white shark, it immediately dove down to 1500ft and swam all the way to Hawaii!

Given this new evidence, does this conclusively prove that Jaws will always come second to the Black Death? The sure answer is a resounding no. Far too much is being made of this incident. We must remember that the victim was only a juvenile white shark. We must remember that as a white shark increases in length its increase in girth becomes disproportionate. It grows considerably nastier and more menacing. Young white shark teeth are designed for grasping slippery fish not murdering large prey. If white sharks have a reason to fear killer whales it is most likely because of their hunting behaviour not because they are the superior lone predator. Killer whales hunt in packs.

Allow me to draw a human analogy.

If I were to meet Evander Holyfield down a dark alley, he would have little to fear. If he was to meet 10 of me down a dark alley (and we had malicious intentions), he would have every right to be fearful. So it is with the white shark and killer whale.

In October 2009, a 10-foot white shark again became the victim of a merciless attack by a larger predator in the waters off Queensland, Australia. In the 1997 incident off California, the killer whale took some time to kill the white shark. Indeed, it appeared to hold it in a state of tonic immobility for some 15 minutes, perhaps wary of reprisals. In the Brisbane incident, the attacker dispensed with such cautious tactics nearly biting the white shark in half with a single bite. The murderer in this case was no Orca. It was an adult white shark (estimated at 20 feet in length). The victim was about the same size as the prey from the 1997 incident. Only this time, the victim was dispatched much more efficiently and clinically.

There is no evidence whatsoever that Orcas predate on fully grown adult white sharks. Indeed, at 20 feet in length, the white shark would be as equally likely to prey on a lone adult Orca.

Chapter 2
Battle for the Land

Polar Bear vs. Siberian Tiger

WHITE POWER

The polar bear is one of the world's largest terrestrial carnivores. It has few rivals for this title. One of those rivals, funnily enough, is another bear, the Kodiak bear, a very large subspecies of brown bear indigenous to Kodiak Island in Alaska.

The average brown bear is considerably smaller than a polar bear. Yet if we compare the size and weight of Kodiak bears and polar bears, it is only a matter of a few pounds that separates them. Polar bears tend to be longer, nose to tail, whilst Kodiak bears tend to be more robustly built. It really depends on the individual. The heaviest recorded Kodiak bear weighed in at 751kg or 1652 lbs for a cage-fat male. In 1960, however, an unconfirmed report came in of a male polar bear exceeding a tonne (1002kg or 2210lbs). Average weights for both these bears, however, approach half a tonne (500kg or 1100lbs).

The representative Daddy in question here, however, is the polar bear. They live in all the polar regions of the northern hemisphere and can be found largely on the sea ice that forms on the edges of land where the northern seas meet the shore. Strangely enough, their Latin name, *Ursus maritimus* translates as 'Sea Bear'. They are tremendous swimmers and prey almost exclusively on marine mammals. They are most at home hunting on the ice but have been known to dive into the surf in pursuit of their prey.

Polar bears seem almost out of place and out of character when being assessed as apex predators. They are simultaneously majestic, and cute and cuddly. I am surely not the only one who wants to take one home and call it Fido, pat it, take it for walks and let it eat burglars. Indeed, bears are closely related to dogs and it is no coincidence that the puppy your friend has just bought "looks like a little bear".

The public perception of bears is somewhat mixed and contradictory. When I was but a nipper there was a show that I used to watch regularly called *Gentle Ben*. It was about a young kid and his adventures with his 'pet'; a rather large bear called Ben. Ben, the hero of the show, was kind and gentle yet heroic and strong; the complete opposite of what we tend to think of when we think of an apex predator.

Bears, like many large predatory animals, were not immune to the *Jaws* phenomenon. *Claws* (so bad it was almost good) and *Grizzly* are but two examples where large brown bears establish a liking for human flesh and go on the rampage, thus requiring human heroes to put an end to their predatory habits.

In quite the same way that domestic dogs and cats seem to dislike each other, if they were ever to interact, bears and big cats wouldn't be the best of friends either. Both are at the top of their respective food chains and something would have to give. In this instance a comparison can be drawn where our friend the polar bear represents Rover, whilst our other friend the Siberian tiger represents Felix.

If I were to bring a polar bear home and call it Fido I might find that my dog biscuit expense account would be rather high. Polar bears are warm-blooded and need to eat regularly to sustain their weight, particularly after awakening from hibernation.

Perhaps the greatest strength of the polar bear lies in its heavy body, especially its huge forelegs. Its legs are topped by its dinner-plate-sized paws, which can deliver tremendously powerful blows to anything unfortunate enough to incur its wrath. The polar bear's chosen delicacy is usually seal meat, caught via two main methods: firstly, using the 'stalk' method, the bear moves slowly, closing in on its prey by relying on its whitish fur for camouflage against the ice, and freezing if the seal looks up. When within approximately twenty to thirty metres, the bear will accelerate to approximately 30mph in order to catch its quarry. Secondly, during the 'still' hunt, the bear will wait, motionless, next to the seal's breathing hole (a hole in the ice where marine mammals will come up to breathe). As the seal surfaces from the water the bear plucks it from the sea and drags it onto land before killing it.

However, these are not the only methods that the polar bear uses. They have been known to dive for their prey, being adept swimmers and able to hold their breath for a couple of minutes under water. Also, polar bears can sniff out a seal den from a considerable distance (in excess of half a mile). Seals make their igloo-like dens underneath thick ice but the incredibly powerful polar bears are undeterred. Standing up on its hind legs and pounding down on the wind packed ice using its forelegs, the bear smashes its way through the ice and straight into the seal dens, dining almost at leisure on the hapless seal pups. Yet polar bears have been known to take far larger prey than seals.

A Russian scientist who spent many years observing polar bear behaviour recounts how they regularly attacked walruses. Walruses are huge relatives of the seals that can weigh up to one and a half tonnes, with huge tusks up to three feet in length in larger individuals. An adult walrus would be an unusual and risky choice of prey item for an adult polar bear. Yet during four years of observation Nikita Ovsyanikov witnessed 35 separate hunting events in which polar bears approached and attempted to seize walruses. Indeed, he stated, "we had polar bears jumping on live walruses and eating walrus carcasses right outside our door". Ovsyanikov stated that little was known about these interactions before his lengthy observations, with only a few scattered reports mentioning walrus carcasses surrounded by polar bear tracks.

Killing a walrus is not easy, even for an adult bear. The majority of hunts lead to panicked walruses escaping into the sea. Ovsyanikov only witnessed successful hunts on walrus calves but as he stated, there could be no doubt that polar bears actively hunt walruses to eat. Not to be outdone, the brown bears from which the polar bears descended have been known to take down similar sized prey in their own native lands. Large brown bears have been observed tackling and successfully killing huge elk, weighing close to a tonne, in North America.

Although polar bears can sometimes congregate in groups in specific areas, they are essentially individual animals. They hunt alone and Ovsyanikov never observed them co-operating to hunt walrus. However, they do co-operate in feeding, by helping to open up the carcass. Chewing through the thick walrus skin can take a polar bear many hours. When finished all that remains is the skin, backbone, skull and several blood-stained polar bears. A fearsome sight indeed; this should remove all notions of a cuddly playful teddy bear, replacing it with the harsh reality of the top carnivores anywhere in the world today.

Not content with walrus, however, polar bears have been known to kill even larger prey. As discussed earlier they will frequently wait at breathing holes in order to catch emerging seals. However, they have also been observed catching whales. Yes - whales. As belugas and narwhals come up to breathe, polar bears sometimes swipe at them, smashing their skulls with a devastating blow from their heavy paws. With the whale stunned, the polar bear then drags the hapless whale onto the ice where it is consumed. Both belugas and narwhals can approach up to sixteen feet in length.

With the big bear actually fishing for whales, can the big kitty-cat pose any serious threat?

POLAR BEAR IN PROFILE

Length Nose to tail - 9 feet average, with a maximum of 11 feet. (3.3 metres)

Weight Average of 500kg, maximum of 750kg

Weaponry A nasty bite, devastating power from both front paws

Speed Up to 30mph

Weaknesses Can be cumbersome in close quarters

Profile Solitary predator, feeding mainly on small pinnipeds but known to take walruses and small whales.

Human Champ Evander Holyfield throws a couple of nice jabs before absorbing a devastating right hook from Mr P Bear. Holyfield drops to the canvass, his neck broken and his head only partially still connected to his shoulders. The bout is a mere 11 seconds old.

STRIPED AGILITY

I have always thought cats have an evil streak. Dogs are loving, caring and loyal. They cheer you up when you are down, cuddle when you are low and provide all-round companionship when the whole world is against you. Cats on the other hand will trick you into a fall sense of security. When they want something they will be the cutest, nicest things in the world but once they have eaten their fill and you have provided them with a bed for the night, their mood changes. Instead of cuddling up next to you on the sofa like Fido, Felix will unleash its claws if you dare to sit down next to it.

Cats must suffer from bad period pains, whatever their sex. One minute they're brushing against your legs, purring away as you stroke them. A minute later, the kitty has gone more than a little sensitive as it bloods you by burying its claws deep into fleshy parts of your anatomy. For the past five years I have been visited at home by a friendly cat. We shared a tin of tuna on the doorstep one summer's evening. I christened him 'Evil' after the cat out of the *Earthworm Jim* cartoon.

I used to have a pet Rottweiler; 100lbs of muscle-bound man's best friend. Man's friend he certainly was; he was only aggressive to a human once when he thought I was being threatened. Cat's friend, on the other hand, he was not. At the very mention of Felix, Jasper would be making a hole in the door to chase them from the garden. Felix would scarper sharpish at the sight of *The Omen*'s devil dog but would still attempt to tease the muscle-bound hound by sitting atop a fence and nonchalantly licking its paws. One day Jasper head-butted the wooden fence, causing Felix to lose his balance and fall on the wrong side. My laughter was cut short by Felix's cries as he was swung back and forth, gripped somehow by the scruff of his neck in the dog's jaws. I hurried outside and ordered Jasper to drop the now shocked and completely frozen-in-fear cat hanging from his jaws. Reluctantly my loyal, obedient and trustworthy friend dropped the cat, which bounded back into life on contact with the ground and disappeared through a hole in the fence. Jasper sulked for the rest of the day.

Similarly, I have never really taken to big cats, particularly African lions. To me at least, they have always seemed icons of pure selfishness. I don't know whether it is the laziness of the big males or the fact that they murder the young that are not of their own direct lineage but African lions have always turned me off somewhat. I have always found myself cheering for their rivals when I watch wildlife documentaries. I am always warmed when a crocodile sees off a lion or a couple of hyenas chase a single lion from a kill. But there is still no denying their place as one of Africa's Daddies. Even a muscle-bound Rottweiler would have to think twice before chasing one of these kitties from their garden. At approximately 400lbs in weight an average African male lion would have nothing to fear from even the largest of domestic dogs. Even though the heaviest mastiff was a robust 300lbs+ it would not possess the mobility or weaponry to deal with a lion of equal weight.

Although a king of Africa the lion is not the king of the cats. That distinction belongs to the tiger. There were eight subspecies of tiger, three of which are now extinct. The other five, unfortunately, remain endangered. The largest of these subspecies, the Daddy cat, is the Siberian tiger. The Siberian tiger is known in Russian legend as 'Amba', meaning 'god and devil'. Males are larger than females, with the record male weighing in at over 800lbs (364kg), although the average weight is around the 600lb (273kg) mark. This is still fifty per cent heavier that an average African lion. Siberian tigers reach nine feet in length; thirteen feet including the tail.

Most Siberian tigers live in the coniferous oak and birch woodlands of eastern Russia where wild pig, wild cattle and deer make up the majority of its diet. Hare, badger and salmon also suffice. Siberian tigers are ambush predators. They will stalk their prey, hiding behind trees, rocks and bushes, getting as close as possible before they pounce. If the tiger misses its prey, it may chase but will rarely catch its intended victim. With smaller prey a single neck bite will sever the spinal cord, whereas a suffocating throat bite is typically used to kill larger prey. The Siberian tiger also boasts the largest canines of any meat-eating animal.

The Siberian tiger is a solitary beast although several adults have been known to congregate and share a kill. Most of their hunting is conducted at night. A Siberian tiger's territory can be as large as 1,200 square miles and as long as the food sources are good, it will remain within its designated area for many years. Only the male will defend his territory against other males.

Tigers do have an unjust reputation as vicious cold-blooded killers. For a start they are warm-blooded and it is thought that only three in every 1000 tigers are man-eaters.

There is no doubt that tigers are fearsome predators. In addition to the prey species mentioned earlier, Siberian tigers are also known to prey on lynx, elk and some small bears. I once remember watching a wildlife documentary where there was a clash of the big cats between a tiger and a leopard. The clash was not captured on film due to the nocturnal behaviour of the cats. Needless to say the tiger was filmed feasting on the remains of the leopard the next day. Also, I have watched programmes before where tigers, in true cat-like fashion, get very moody around (admittedly domesticated) small Indian elephants. However, despite the tiger flashing its claws and the elephant retreating, the tiger never actually looked like it could actually take down the elephant. It was simply being moody like all cats are and the elephant simply couldn't be bothered with the moaning Felix.

Yet rumours do abound of tigers attacking young rhinoceroses and elephants. Also, tigers in the Ranthambore reserve in northwest India have been reported to have attacked, killed and eaten crocodiles. However, the size and scale of their crocodilian victims was not specified. Tigers do not really match the polar bear in taking prey that is far bigger and heavier than them. Could this be because walruses and beluga whales are not indigenous to the tiger's habitat or are they simply not capable of taking down prey that large?

Predator Deathmatch

SIBERIAN TIGER IN PROFILE

Length	Nose to tail – maximum 13 feet (4 metres)
Weight	Weight 270kg, maximum of 400kg (880lbs)
Weaponry	Retractable claws and large canines - nasty
Speed	Up to 35mph
Weaknesses	Low body weight
Profile	Solitary predator, feeding mainly on smaller mammals. Rumoured to attack small elephants and crocodiles.
Human Champ	Evander Holyfield comes out aggressively but immediately sustains a nasty cut and broken ribs courtesy of those retractable claws. Holyfield covers up on the ground but receives a terrible mauling. After 32 seconds of the bout Holyfield's spinal cord is severed due to a crushing bite to the back of the neck.

BIG FIGHT BUILD-UP

The big white bear has to enter this match-up as a big favourite. At half the weight of its opponent and with devastating power coming from the bear's front paws, the big pussy has its work cut out. The sea bear is a proven and regular killer of very large prey; prey that is considerably larger than itself. When the kitty goes hunting for fish it doesn't happen to catch adult whales with its large claws, a feat achieved by adult polar bears.

However, we should not be writing off the tiger too soon. It too possesses tremendous strength and has perhaps the greater weaponry of the two combatants. Also, claims abound of the tiger taking prey larger than itself. Yet in all cases where the tiger is claimed to have taken prey larger than itself, there is little evidence to support it taking adult specimens. The tide again begins to turn back towards the sea bear.

Theoretically there is no logical reason why a Siberian tiger and a polar bear should not come face to face in real life. Polar bears roam vast areas of the Arctic, including the Siberian tundra, the haunt of the Siberian tiger. However, encounters are unlikely. Firstly, the Siberian tiger is endangered; there are very few specimens actually left in the wild and furthermore, the bears are more likely to keep to the coastal areas hence their 'sea bear' nickname. Most of their prey does, after all, come from the sea.

This is not to say that our two terrestrial Daddies have not clashed. However, I for one am not aware of it and would be fascinated to hear the stories of any claimed encounters.

In summary, the polar bear will go into this bout as a heavy betting favourite. However, the Siberian tiger is said to have taken to heart comments from some quarters that the grizzly bear should be fighting in his place. His best strategy will be to utilise his weapons whilst keeping out of the way of those devastating front paws. If the tiger can get a few unanswered swipes in early this bout might just go his way. Either way it will be an intriguing clash.

SECONDS OUT

The two combatants approach and circle, neither diverting its gaze from the other. Suddenly the polar bear makes a rush at the Siberian tiger. The tiger raises itself up onto its hind legs, making a grab at the polar bear with its front paws. The polar bear does likewise raising itself to its full height of nearly ten feet. For a moment it looks like the combatants will wrestle each other in a contest of strength. But this is no contest of strength. The bear throws the tiger several feet to the side.

The cat lands heavily but appears more shocked than hurt. As it hits the ground it instantly regains its feet and instinctively turns to run. However, in this caged arena there is nowhere to hide.

The striped cat slinks into a corner, attempting to make itself as small as possible as if trying to make itself invisible. The polar bear stalks towards the tiger; slowly, methodically, purposely. As the bear nears the tiger, the caged kitty pounces, taking the bear by surprise and slashing at its midriff with its claws; the bear is bloodied, an ever-growing patch of red staining its brilliant white fur.

Yet rather than press home this initiative with another wave, the kitty is still wary of the great bear's power, again retreating to a corner. There is an uneasy and 'actionless' minute. The bear prowls back and forth, up and down as if contemplating its next move, the tiger remains in its corner.

For a moment a stalemate looks possible but then hunger again drives the bear forward. As it approaches, the cat again lunges outwards. This time, however, the result is very different. The bear unleashes a devastating right hand catching the cat just behind the right shoulder. The bear sustains another cut, but the tiger has taken a big shot and drops, stunned.

The bear, unlike the tiger, offers no mercy and presses home its attack. The tiger again tries to retreat but limps from its injury. The bear swipes at the cat, hitting its target and weakening it further. The bear moves in on its opponent, which now has limited mobility.

A mauling ensues, the bear wading in with both powerful front paws and finally its teeth to despatch its latest victim. The tiger puts up a spirited defence once it has been cornered and bloods the bear a fair bit more. Ultimately, however, the bear asserts its authority as the terrestrial Daddy carnivore.

Verdict: Ultimately, the bear emerges bloodied but victorious; it was just too big, too heavy and too strong for the king of the kitties.

POST-FIGHT ANALYSIS

As the hysteria from the polar bear's victory dies down and the body of the great cat is removed for burial, the organisers of this match-up need to take a long hard look at their choice of combatants to contest this vacant title. The new champion has a queue of potential opponents all with CVs that are arguably superior to that of the Siberian tiger. The managers of Mr Lion, Mr Grizzly, Mr Bengal Tiger, Mr Kodiak bear and Mr Liger are all making a lot of noise in favour of their charges; not to mention the manager of Mr Crocodile. By beating the Siberian tiger does the polar bear really deserve the title of Daddy? There does appear to be some historical evidence that may suggest otherwise....

Firstly we need to point out that strictly speaking, the Siberian tiger is not the largest feline in the world. This title actually belongs to the liger, the offspring of a lion father and a tiger mother. As big cat hybridisations go this is a relatively common combination, occurring quite often in captivity by accident. Ligers visually share characteristics of both parents. Their `vocabulary` is made up of both lion and tiger sounds and confusion between the lion and the tiger sides of their personality is quite often noted by handlers.

No official scientific name exists for hybrid animals such as these. Hybrid animals, whatever their species, are nearly always infertile and therefore have not developed into a separate lineage. However, some female ligers have been fertile and have bred with normal lions or tigers. Yet to date there have been no fertile male ligers.

Incidentally, when a lion mother and tiger father reproduce, the offspring is known as a tigon. Tigons seem to show a tendency towards dwarfism; ligers on the other hand display what is known as 'hybrid vigour'. This means that the offspring grow much larger and at a more rapid rate than their parents. Ligers are the largest felid in the world and can stand twelve feet tall on their hind legs. Ligers may weigh in at half a tonne and there are rumours of even heavier specimens, although these are most likely to be 'cage fat'; that is, well fed by their human handlers. In the wild it is highly unlikely a liger would get that heavy because it would never be able to catch its prey.

However, despite rivalling the polar bear in size and weight, the liger is unlikely to fair any better than the Siberian tiger and probably not as well. All ligers have been bred and raised in captivity; they have no need to hunt or fight. Their handlers have noted that ligers have quite a gentle and easy-going disposition. This kitty, whilst possessing the physique and looking every bit the part, is unlikely to be able to deliver the goods in the hour of need. The polar bear wins by an easy stoppage.

There is no doubt that the heaviest tiger is considerably heavier than the heaviest lion. Also, few would dispute that it is a better predator and hunter than a lion. This is slightly spurious as lions hunt in groups and tigers are solitary. In the one-on-one hunting stakes, the tiger would likely be more successful and be able to bring down larger prey. Yet this does not necessarily make it a superior *fighter* when compared to a lion. Indeed, there is some historical evidence to suggest that it is not.

The likelihood of a lion and tiger encounter in the wild is virtually non-existent as their natural habitats do not overlap. It has been stated that Gir National Park and Sanctuary in India houses both tigers and lions (Asiatic lion), but the lion actually holds it as an exclusive range.

Despite the fact that the two cats' paths do not cross in the wild, their paths have been engineered to cross, particularly in the fighting pit. Three films are rumoured to exist of lion and tiger fights. The first in captivity was set up to entertain a prince and took place in the pit of a palace compound. The film showed that the tiger was at an immediate disadvantage. Tigers use a throat grip as their main killing technique and the thick mane of the lion acted as a protective buffer, preventing the tiger from gaining a hold on the throat. The tiger, however, had no special protection and was more open to attack. In this fight the tiger was killed. No mention is made of the subspecies of tiger or the size and weight of both cats.

Another piece of film, supposedly dating back to the 1930s, is alleged to have been shot in the Gir region of India. Again the tiger was the loser but very little information can actually be found on this film.

A third film rumoured to exist shows a Korean pit fight between a lion and a tiger. The fight was supposedly staged in a caged arena and the tiger is said to have injured the lion's hind leg. This disabled the lion long enough for the tiger to apply a hold on the lion's neck, which was subsequently shaken, resulting in damage to the lion's spine. Although suffering some claw and bite marks, the tiger emerged victorious. Again the size and weights of the combatants prove elusive.

There was a great deal of lion and tiger pit-fighting in Korea before 1960. Historic reports say that the lion was difficult to beat due to protection afforded by its mane. The lion was typically the victor.

The Koreans normally used the Siberian tiger and despite its size, it put in some poor performances, often showing an unwillingness to fight. Historical documents from ancient Rome also seem to support this. Lions were more popular in the gladiatorial arena as they put on an excellent fighting display, whereas tigers were often reluctant to enter into battle, simply retreating when placed in with lions.

A fair degree of expert opinion is that the modern male lion has no equal amongst other big cats when it comes to its fighting ability. Lions evolved as fighters and amongst their pride their primary job is to protect their females from marauding males who would assume control of their pride and kill their young. An adult male lion spends much of his life in combat situations and nature has supported the lion with the evolution of a protective mane.

The tiger, on the other hand, has no feline rival as a predator, but shies away from an open fight. The tiger is a lone predator and fighting can lead to injury, which in turn can lead to starvation. Lions on the other hand act as a group and injured members can rely on the strength of the pride. Tigers have no such luxury and instinctively back away from dangerous combat situations so that they may hunt another day.

Predation for food does not correlate with performance in battle. It is a common misapprehension that being the better solitary hunter automatically equals being a better fighter. This rule applies itself throughout the entire animal kingdom. For example, the giant Tarantula spider is frequently preyed upon by the Tarantula-eating wasp, which lies in wait for the big spider, stinging and subsequently paralysing the big arachnid often before it is even aware of the wasp's presence. The wasp will then lay its young in the paralysed spider's body, allowing the young wasps to eat the Tarantula from within. The wasp will dig a burrow, wait for the Tarantula to approach and spring out with its killer sting, catching the spider unawares.

However, one disgruntled Tarantula-loving researcher set about equalising the imbalance. Collecting specimens of both the Tarantula and the Tarantula-eating wasp, he placed them both in a sealed tank. This time aware of the wasp, the Tarantula turned the wasp into prey. Despite being an excellent predator and able to despatch a Tarantula bigger than itself in a natural environment, the wasp proved to be less effective at open fighting. It was nowhere near as effective when its ambush advantage was removed.

This would appear to be the case with lions and tigers. Yet let us not write the tiger off too soon. In the case of a lion attacking another maned lion, many have learnt not to attack the throat. They have learnt to attack the legs. This is purely learnt behaviour and the tiger would not know how to use this technique, never having had the need. If tigers and lions were to interact regularly however, then surely the tiger would learn this. This turns the balance of the fight outcome towards the tiger.

Furthermore, the Koreans, disappointed with the performance of the Siberian tiger in the pit, began to extend their search for a tiger with a more vicious nature. Eventually they settled for Bengal tigers from the Nepal valley region. Bengal tigers are close to the Siberian tigers in weight, typically weighing in at around 500lbs. Within the Bengal tiger the Koreans were said to have found a ferocious cat, which attacked violently and relentlessly, winning in most of its clashes with lions. Strangely, this aggressive tendency was confined to tigers from only one very small area. It is thought that this high level of aggression developed after a large number of tigers became cut off in a relatively small forest. This would greatly increase the frequency of territorial confrontation between tigers, and competition over the small amount of prey would intensify. The result would be a tiger with extremely heightened aggression but still crucially outweighing a lion. With its aggression matched and giving away weight, it is understandable that the lion faired less well against tigers from this particular area.

Also, in the 1930s the Maharajah of Gwalior carried out an interesting experiment. He imported three pairs of African lions as breeding stock and decided to release them into the Shivpuri-Sheopur forest, which covers 1000 square miles. A walled enclosure allowed for acclimatisation within which the lions thrived and bred for four years, after which they were released into the local forests. The lions spread out but were apparently mauled and killed by the local tigers.

In defence of the lions they were out of their natural habitat and had been hand fed for four years, no doubt eroding much of their hunting skill. Wild male lions also face competition from challengers on a frequent basis. The captive lions would not have faced this, adding further to their ring rust. Finally, when faced with angry tigers defending their territory, the lions' lack of fighting practice during the previous four years ultimately led to their death (somewhat understandably).

Quite commonly the lion versus tiger debate focuses on the Siberian tiger because of its superior size and weight. The organisers of such clashes, however, are frequently mistaken in believing that the large size of the Siberian tiger means a more aggressive animal and therefore a better fighter. The fact is that the Siberian tiger lacks the aggression of its cousin from the Asian subcontinent, which in turn lacks the aggression and ferocity of a lion.

Also, whilst the Siberian tiger is slightly longer and heavier than the Bengal, the difference is less than popularly thought. Much of the Siberian tiger's extra bulk is fat to keep it warm in the Siberian forests and a false impression is generated by their longer, thicker coats.

The tiger has a longer body and is usually more powerful in the back legs, having evolved for greater speed and bounding to surprise prey. The lion usually stands slightly taller at the shoulder and has a larger head and more power in the forequarters, paradoxically making him a poorer predator.

In conclusion, it appears that the lion comes out ahead of the tiger in the fighting stakes. However, the most aggressive tiger would probably be more than a match for the most aggressive lion.

So, is the Daddy polar bear under threat from either a Bengal tiger or a lion? Again we can look at some historical factual evidence to evaluate this.

The Siberian tiger does share the forest with a powerful neighbour in the form of the Siberian brown bear, a close relative of the grizzly. It lacks the ferocity of its North American cousin, but big males can still grow towards 1500lbs at the upper limit. Tigers do predate on small bears, but would generally avoid bears of a size equal to their own. However, a 1000lb bear has little if anything to fear from an adult tiger. Eventually these two huge animals will run into each other. The remains of two large adult male tigers were discovered in the year 2000. The remains bore the hallmarks of brown bear predation.

What if a Bengal tiger or a Lion were to have a pit fight with a brown bear? Would they fare any better? The answer is that they probably wouldn't.

The Californians of the late 19th century staged well documented pit fights between grizzly bears and Spanish bulls. Whilst grizzlies are active predators, they are also omnivorous meaning that their diet does not consist purely of meat. They do take down large prey when the opportunity presents itself or hunger drives them to it.

The grizzly bear has evolved enormous bone and muscle density. This is in contrast to big cat biology. The large felines have evolved powerful elastic muscles over a lighter frame with a low density bone structure, enabling them to hunt down prey more efficiently.

Anyway, when the Spanish bulls were wheeled in to combat the grizzlies, the contests became so much of a mismatch that betting was called off. Using their immensely powerful front paws as a club, the grizzlies shattered the unfortunate bull's skull or shoulder bones with ease, thus ending the contest.

Having no competition for the grizzly, the Californians eventually brought over some African lions to raise the stakes. The fiercest of the adult male lions was sent in to try and topple the grizzly. The lion was known for bravely charging in and looking the part. However, to the dismay of the Californians the grizzly dispatched the African lion with almost as much ease as he had the Spanish bulls. The enormously strong bone-density and power of the grizzly meeting the low-density skull of the lion, which could not get close enough to apply its windpipe-lock, rendered the contest yet another mismatch. It is hard to imagine how even the most fierce Bengal tiger would have fared any better.

Thus, if there is going to be a contender to the polar bear's crown it has to come from a subspecies of brown bear such as the grizzly, particularly noted for its aggression. The polar bear does tend to be slightly larger than the grizzly, having a thinner, longer and more delicate skull, along with its narrower forequarters: this streamlining is an adaptation for its aquatic lifestyle. The grizzly has a shorter, thicker neck, heavier skull and more powerful shoulder structure, but it is a fair bit shorter than the polar bear. However, the claws of the grizzly have evolved as tremendous digging tools and are unmatched at opening carcasses. Six-inch claws are relatively common compared to the small two-inch hook like claws of the polar bear.

Polar bears are incredibly successful predators, often taking down prey much larger than themselves. Grizzlies on the other hand, by comparison, are relatively poor predators. However, they have been known to take adult elk, moose, caribou and muskox; again, prey that is larger than them.

To really decide who the Daddy is on the land, big cats simply do not come into the equation. The polar bear must defend against a large subspecies of brown bear. The betting in this instance would be fairly even.

Chapter 3
Terrestrial Battle of the Ages
Who's the Daddy Dinosaur?

TYRANT LIZARD KING

Deciding on the victor for this section may prove difficult as we have very little to go on. There are no videotapes of prehistoric predatory behaviour, no historical evidence of pit fighting, not even a solitary eyewitness to fall back on. When choosing the Daddy dinosaur all we have to go on are their fossils. By their very nature, these are not going to provide us with as much information and data as we have on all the animals discussed so far. Despite this, we must boldly step forward and begin a contest of elimination in search of the mightiest predator amongst the terrible lizards.

Dinosaurs have always fascinated me. As far back as I can remember I have collected plastic models of every kind of dinosaur imaginable. Between the ages of about six and ten it seemed that everybody my age had a dinosaur fetish and several of them collected models. The coolest kid had the latest model. At this tender age I and two other dinosaur fetishists (weather permitting) would gather in the largest garden and put all of our combined dinosaur models into one big pile. We would then select in turn our chosen dinosaurs, enabling us to select dinosaurs we did not actually own ourselves for the ensuing game. Having selected our 30-odd dinosaurs each, we would then spread them out around the garden, each of us giving a running commentary as we staged our own personal Dinosaur Daddy Contest to find the ultimate winner. Many a long summer's day was spent in this manner during my childhood. Between us an almost unhealthy knowledge of dinosaur statistics – weights, measures and weaponry – had been assembled and could be recited at a moments notice. Dinosaur posters adorned our bedroom walls, dinosaur books slotted neatly into shelves, and dinosaur Top Trumps formed an integral part of our life.

When I was ten years old my parents moved me 200 miles away from my happy environment and I had to try and begin a new. Like the African lions released into the Gir forest (see previous chapter) I felt lonely and confused, separated from my dinosaur-loving, gamebook reading, card-playing companions.

Several years later when I had gained some independence I tracked down these old friends of mine and we remain in touch today. However, whereas they had grown out of their dinosaur fetish, I was still trapped in a lost world. Dinosaurs still haunt my thoughts, my model collection continues to grow and much to my girlfriend's annoyance, my favourite models fill every spare windowsill or mantelpiece in our house.

Dinosaur knowledge has progressed handsomely since my fascination began nearly thirty years ago. A new dinosaur species is discovered almost weekly. When I was but a nipper *Tyrannosaurus rex* was the undisputed Daddy. If us kids had a favourite dinosaur, the tyrant lizard king (Latin translation), was top of most lists. He was, after all, the meanest, nastiest, most fearsome predator ever to have roamed the earth. When playing Top Trumps, *T. rex* was the only card to achieve a carnivore eight score. His nearest rival, *Allosaurus*, could only manage a carnivore seven score. He was the ultimate mean dude. Nobody could touch the *T. rex* and all the other dinosaurs lived in fear of him.

Predator Deathmatch

When I was about eight, one of my fellow dinosaur compadres came into school one day and announced that a new meat-eating dinosaur had been discovered that was bigger than *T. rex*. I remember at the time feeling cold, hit for six, almost like a good friend had just died (the next time I felt like that was when Marvelous Marvin Hagler was robbed against Sugar Ray Leonard). On that occasion my friend had read a newspaper report that was in error. However, since then several meat-eating dinosaurs have come forth to challenge the claims of the mighty *Tyrannosaurus rex* as the undisputed king of the dinosaurs. Most of the biggest and fearsome meat-eaters are what are known as 'theropods'. Theropods had many general characteristics: they were carnivores, tended to have blade-like teeth, were long-legged, bipedal, slender and quick. They had three walking toes on their hind feet and the outer fingers on their hand were either reduced in size or completely lost. Basically, a theropod is a huge walking skull that can bite you in half with ease.

Before choosing who will represent the dinosaurs in the ultimate battle of terrestrial carnivores we will take a brief look at each of the contenders in turn. Many dinosaurs have a claim on this title. To list them all and back up their claims would require another book in itself. Therefore, in the greatest boxing traditions, I have compiled a list of the top ten contenders that I think would have a legitimate right to challenge *Tyrannosaurus rex* for its title, and then give a brief discussion of their merits:

Reigning Champion: *Tyrannosaurus rex*

> *Giganotosaurus*
> *Carcharodontosaurus*
> *Megaraptor*
> *Spinosaurus*
> *Tarbosaurus*
> *Acrocanthosaurus*
> *Allosaurus*
> *Torvosaurus*
> *Megalosaurus*
> *Deinocheirus*

Starting with the number ten contender and rising:

Deinocheirus Very little is known about this dinosaur and many experts would be surprised to see it as a contender for the title. However, on the basis of what *is* known about it (or perhaps not known about it), it scrapes into the top ten as a dark horse. Discovered in Mongolia in 1970, 'deinocheirus' means 'terrible hand'. This is apt because the hands and the arms are the only parts of this dinosaur so far discovered. It is known only from two

huge eight-foot-long arms with ten-inch claws. The arms are similar to those of Ornithomimids, although the digits and claws are more curved. Ornithomimids were ostrich-like dinosaurs with small heads, flexible necks, toothless beaks, elongated arms, slim hind limbs and grasping hands with three powerful fingers. Because of their lower leg bone and structure it is likely that these dinosaurs were capable of great speeds. However, we cannot be sure that the rest of *Deinocherius* (actually an ornithomimiosaur) accurately resembled an ornithomimid. Yet, assuming it was, and scaling it up from more complete ornithomimid skeletons, it is possible that *Deinocherius* could have reached quite a length, and its ten-inch claws would have been dangerous weapons. This would make it on a similar scale to even the largest theropods. However, it is likely to have been much lighter in build and it is hard to see it exceeding much over three tonnes in weight.

Megalosaurus Or 'big lizard', was the first ever dinosaur to be formally named, originating from England in 1826. Early restorations from that era incorrectly showed it to be quadrupedal and it did have unusually short forelimbs, even for a theropod. In my dinosaur youth I always understood *Megalosaurus* to be like a small *T. rex* (in the region of 30 feet in length) and a lot lighter in build. Over the years many new species of theropod have been unceremoniously dumped into the megalosaur bin and it would appear that palaeontologists (fossil experts) have a fair amount of sorting to do in this arena. However, some of the megalosaurids approach the size of *T. rex*, including *Megalosaurus ingens* of Tanzania and *Bahariasaurus* from Egypt and Algeria. The famous American palaeontologist Bob Bakkar has gone on record to say he feels that the megalosaurs were the Daddy dinosaur. He bases much of his argument on a broken rib bone he has from a megalosaur that he believes came from an animal larger then *T. rex*.

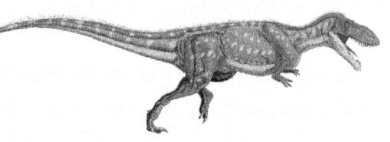

Torvosaurus Or 'savage lizard', is a fairly recent theropod discovery from 1979. It was only about 33 feet in length, but was unusually bulky for its size and is thought to have exceeded five tonnes in weight.

Allosaurus translates as 'different lizard' and was first discovered way back in 1877. It was a large theropod from the Jurassic period (pre dating *T. rex*, which came from the later Cretaceous period). *Allosaurus* is quite common from the fossil record, but like the megalosaurs, suffers from some suspicious sorting by palaeontologists. As a kid I always understood *Allosaurus* to be smaller than *T. rex* but larger than *Megalosaurus*, weighing in at around four tonnes, compared to two tonnes for *Megalosaurus*. However, some allosaurs appear to have reached very large sizes. One excavated in Oklahoma in 1934 was said to

have reached a total body length of 42 feet and been built on bigger lines than the tyrannosaurids, also having arms twice as long.

Acrocanthosaurus Or 'high spine lizard', was first discovered in 1950. This large animal had long vertebrae along its back, possibly forming a sail. The vertebral spines were eight to twelve inches high along the neck and tail, possibly up to twenty inches along the back. It was once classified as a spinosaur since, like *Spinosaurus* it had  long vertebral spines. But the rest of the animal is little like *Spinosaurus* even the 'fin' is different. It is thought that it may be a late allosaur, having evolved from an early species of allosaur. It reached up to 40 feet in length and weighed up to four tonnes.

Tarbosaurus, meaning 'alarming lizard', is the largest predator to come out of Asia. We are  now climbing higher up the ranks and starting to pose a serious threat to the tyrant lizard king. *Tarbosaurus* would appear to be a cousin of *T. rex*. What is known about *Tarbosaurus* comes from a Mongolian expedition dating back to 1946. *Tarbosaurus* is very closely related to *Tyrannosaurus rex* and of comparable size. However, since it was discovered the remains of *Tarbosaurus* have not been easily accessible to western palaeontologists. Indeed, it has led one researcher to comment that "it is diabolically unfortunate that the majority of Gobi tyrannosaurid (including *Tarbosaurus*) specimens have never been illustrated in print" and "despite the demise of communism, information about Mongolian tyrannosaurids remain a state secret". Furthermore, this same researcher, on being able to study a *Tarbosaurus* skull, added that he would almost feel confident enough to call it *T. rex*. That is, *Tarbosaurus* has been erroneously identified as a different dinosaur when in fact it is one and the same as *T. rex*.

Spinosaurus In a similar vein to *Jaws*, the movie *Jurassic Park* has a lot to answer for. The third one included the screen debut of the spine lizard – *Spinosaurus*. In the movie *Spinosaurus* clashed with an adult *T. rex* and won! *Spinosaurus* is indeed a worthy opponent and has been estimated in body length at up to sixty feet. It was possibly the longest and heaviest theropod, but it was much lighter in build when compared to *T. rex*. As remarkable as its length was, even more interesting was the huge sail along the back, formed by long vertebral spines of up to six feet in height in places. The exact nature of this bizarre sail is not known. It is thought that even at fifty feet in length, *Spinosaurus* would probably only have weighed in at around seven tonnes. Also, its somewhat elongated crocodilian skull would probably have been most adept at fishing rather than bone-

crushing or slicing. The scene depicted in the movie would be an unlikely one.

Megaraptor *Jurassic Park* again has something to answer for here. Generations of youngsters who have grown up with the movie believe that *Velociraptors* were six feet tall and lethal to all but the largest dinosaurs. In truth, *Velociraptors* would have stood about three feet tall and weighed about 100lbs. They still would have been fairly lethal, and could have tackled prey much larger than themselves, particularly if they hunted in packs. In isolation they will have posed no threat to a large theropod. However, *Velociraptor-like* dinosaurs did grow a lot larger. *Deinonychus* grew to the size depicted in the movie and there were some raptors that grew considerably larger. A similar, but completely unrelated creature - an allosauroid (specifically, a neovenatorid carcharodontosaur) was *Megaraptor*, or 'big raider'. Described in 1998, it was about twenty-five feet long in total body length. It had a fourteen-inch sickle claw, with which it could probably inflict an enormous amount of damage. Raptors were fairly lightweight and nimble and even *Megaraptor* would be hard pushed to exceed a single tonne. Pound for pound, the raptors would have been unrivalled but would the king raptor have enough weaponry and agility to seriously take on the tyrant lizard?

Carcharodontosaurus Or 'shark-toothed lizard' was first discovered in the 1920s but the remains housed in a Berlin museum were destroyed during the Second World War. A much more recent expedition in the 1990s found a specimen some fifteen per cent larger than the lost wartime remains. These new finds show that this African theropod was a massive predator and a serious rival to *T. rex*. Initially, it was thought that the newly unearthed *Carcharodontosaurus* specimen had the largest head of any theropod, although it seems that the reconstructed skull was too long. That accolade has been most recently attributed to its close relative from South America, giganotosaurus. However, *Carcharodontosaurus* is still thought to come in at around the forty feet mark in body length and weigh in at around seven to eight tonnes.

Giganotosaurus Discovered in Argentina in 1993, the 'giant southern lizard' is widely gaining acceptance as the largest carnivorous dinosaur known to science. *Giganotosaurus* is very

similar in appearance and proportions to the number two contender, *Carcharodontosaurus*. The specimen discovered in 1993 is slightly longer than Sue, the largest *T. rex* on record. Also, *Giganotosaurus* had a more robust bone structure than *T. rex*, suggesting that it was heavier. Its skull was longer and narrower than that of *T. rex*, with dagger-like serrated teeth. Perhaps like a modern great white shark, its teeth suggest that *Giganotosaurus* would bite its prey then back off, waiting for its victim to bleed and weaken before pressing home its attack. It is estimated that *Giganotosaurus* would weigh in at around eight tonnes. Additionally, some new discoveries from the same area in which *Giganotosaurus* was unearthed are threatening the newly crowned size king. It is unclear yet whether these new specimens are more *Giganotosaurus* or a new species. It also remains unclear precisely how large these new specimens are.

Tyrannosaurus rex So has the king been dethroned? Well, for many years *T. rex* was considered to be the largest predator to roam the earth. It would now appear that rival dinosaurs were at least as large as *T. rex*; possibly larger. However, it is worth stressing that *T. rex* and *Giganotosaurus* were not all that closely related. *T. rex* was the later, more evolved model of the two; more intelligent by half (literally – its brain case was over 50 per cent larger). They had very different skulls. *T. rex* did not have the serrated daggers of *Giganotosaurus*. Instead, *T. rex* had large, strong, blunt crushers. It had a much wider skull, a much stronger jaw and far greater bone-crushing ability. It is also worth noting that just as *Giganotosaurus* begins celebrating its ascendancy and crowning as the biggest carnivore to walk the earth, a 1997 discovery from Montana, USA, may throw a further spanner in the works. This discovery may be about to return *T. rex* to the top in the size stakes. Still being prepared, this specimen seems to be considerably larger than Sue, the previous largest *T. Rex*. So, the tyrant lizard may still be king after all.

In assessing the Daddy of the carnivorous dinosaurs we can see that *T. rex* has many legitimate challengers, not all of whom have been mentioned here. *Dynamosaurus* was another counterpart from China, which was in a similar size league. An allosaur from China named *Yangchuanosaurus* may have been the largest non-tyrannosaurid ever. Yet we must also ask does bigger mean better fighter? We have seen already with the big cats this is not necessarily the case.

Unlike with the big cats, however, we will never be able to test this unless someone invents a time machine so that natural historians can go back and observe predatory behaviour. Therefore, we have to make the best of what we have and in the case of a lot of dinosaur discoveries, that is not a lot at all. An awful lot of information is frequently written about a dinosaur on the basis of only a handful of bone fragments. Consequently, new dinosaur discoveries frequently mean that current scientific 'knowledge' is constantly being rewritten.

EDITOR'S NOTE: The dinosaur pictures on the previous few pages are - like the photographs used elsewhere in the book, and the images on p.60, and 78 - public domain from Wikipedia Commons. Thanks guys...

Some scientists have postulated that *T. rex* was more of a scavenger than a hunter. Given its prowess for bone-crushing, it has been likened to a hyena (today's big bone-crusher). However, despite the hyena's known scavenging habits it is also an active hunter and a very good one at that. It is hard to imagine that *T. rex* was a pure scavenger. More likely it was an active hunter that frequently scavenged by chasing lesser carnivores from one of their kills. But the question remains could it have chased all dinosaurs from a kill or were there some that would fight back and chase off *T. rex*? Let us imagine some prehistoric encounters and revisit our contenders.

Firstly *Deinocheirus*: apart from its huge arms we have very little to go on here. Interestingly, another huge-armed dinosaur lived in the same region at the same time as *Deinocheirus*, called *Therizinosaurus*. This animal had seven-foot arms and had the largest claws of any known animal (approaching three feet!). *Therizinosaurus* discoveries have been more complete than *Deinocheirus*. It exceeded thirty feet in total length and much debate has ensued about the use of its claws. It has been suggested that the huge claws were for grasping and tearing apart large victims or alternatively, for ripping open giant termite nests. *Therizinosaurus* had a weak skull lacking in teeth and it would appear that it was herbivorous and does not make the grade as a contender. Future *Deinocheirus* discoveries will have to provide us with more ammunition than *Therizinosaurus*. In all likelihood *Therizinosaurus* and *Deinocheirus* were probably omnivorous, eating both prey and plants. Even if *Deinocheirus* did exceed 60 feet (and this is debateable) it is unlikely to have had the weight or the power to fight off an adult *T. rex*. If it defended its kill, it would probably have ended up as lunch.

Megaraptor would have proved more of a genuine contender. Raptors have traditionally been viewed as small, swift, vicious and cunning hunters, as opposed to brutal and strong. *Megaraptor* shakes this belief up a little. However, even though *Megaraptor* is scaled up somewhat from the unrelated *Velociraptors* made famous in *Jurassic Park*, it would still be considered rapid, nimble and explosive when compared to *T. rex*. Furthermore, its weaponry can be conservatively described as lethal. Its fourteen-inch sickle claw would readily rip large chunks of flesh from whatever it sank into. If *Megaraptors* hunted in packs there would probably be few, if any, isolated dinosaurs that could resist attacks. Alone, *Megaraptor* would still be a fearsome hunter and a tremendous fighter. Yet against a *T. rex,* it is likely to have been outweighed by some five or six times. I would compare it to a great welterweight fighting a good heavyweight. During the early rounds the welterweight is likely to point score successfully without causing any lasting damage. However, the moment the heavyweight lands a telling shot it would be all over. The welterweight would have to be exceptionally gifted to avoid taking a shot for the duration of the fight. Similarly, I see *Megaraptor* darting in and out using its sickle claw to rip chunks from *T. rex*. Despite suffering injuries, eventually *T. rex* will gain a grip of *Megaraptor* with those bone crushing jaws and it's goodnight *Megaraptor.* The result of this match up became conclusive upon the discovery of a complete front limb from *Megaraptor*. This showed that the giant claw actually came from the first finger of the hand. The hands were unusually elongated, bearing sickle-shaped claws. *Megaraptor* would have no doubt still possessed an impressive sickle claw on its feet but probably not as impressive as we once thought. Any hope it had against *T. rex* just evaporated.

All the remaining contenders are large theropods, similar in design to *T. rex*. With regards to *Allosaurus* and *Megalosaurus*, it is difficult to see how even the largest specimens could rival the largest *T. rex* in size. They may have had an edge on speed but they would lack the powerful bite of a *T. rex*. Even Bob Bakker conceded that his mega-megalosaur would lose to *T. rex* in open terrain (although he contends not in forest). *Acrocanthosaurus* was like a slightly scaled up *Allosaurus* and again can only be seen as the loser against *T. rex*. *Torvosaurus* is interesting: short, stocky and powerful. Ultimately, however, it was smaller and lighter than *T. rex*, which again defends its crown. *Tarbosaurus* is a serious threat but so little information is available on those 1946 discoveries that it is difficult to assess its chances. It would appear to be like a brother to *T. rex* but politics is preventing *Tarbosaurus* getting its true shot at the title. Maybe a future reappraisal of its remains will shed further light.

Spinosaurus is basking in its new-found celebrity status. Those in the know have long been aware of its capabilities but *Jurassic Park 3* has elevated its kudos. A few people have now asked me "what was that thing that killed *T. rex* in the movie?" I'm afraid, however, that the computer animators have been getting carried away with themselves. *Spinosaurus* may have been longer than *T. rex* but it was lighter in build. Furthermore, its jaws were clearly more suited to catching large fish than bringing down large dinosaurs. Its bite would not have been all that destructive. *T. rex* would make mincemeat of *Spinosaurus*. This, contrary to what moviemakers would have us believe, would be heavily weighted in favour of *T. rex*.

To clarify this, allow me to draw a human analogy. I am slightly heavier than Manny Pacquiao (widely regarded as the finest pound for pound boxer in the world in 2009). I have a background in explosive power sports. By conventional measure, I am likely to be not only slightly bigger, but stronger. However, were we to step into a boxing ring, Manny's punch precision, timing, hand speed and ring generalship would soon overwhelm any strength advantage I might have. His boxing skills are the equivalent of having a *T Rex* skull (compared to my elongate *Spinosaurus* fish-catching skull). It remains something of an enigma why a specialist fish eater should grow into such a large predatory dinosaur. However, unless the tactic was simply to sit on him *Spinosaurus* was no *T Rex* killer. It simply lacked the weaponry to be a truly devastating predator of large prey.

This leaves us with two genuine contenders to the throne in *Carcharodontosaurus* and *Giganotosaurus*. As *Giganotosaurus* is thought to be the slightly larger of these two let us deal with it first. *Giganotosaurus* was undoubtedly a huge predator. It was a similar length to *T. rex* and probably about fifteen to twenty per cent heavier between specimens of similar length. *Giganotosaurus* had slashing serrated blades for teeth, against *T. rex's* bone-crushing spikes. Recent discoveries suggest that both predators may have roamed in packs or small family groups. Never mind a fight; this could be the ultimate war! The key question is whether *Giganotosaurus* could have made use of its extra weight? Unfortunately for *Giganotosaurus*, *T. rex* comes back in other areas. *T. rex* was more intelligent and probably quicker on its feet. The skull of *Giganotosaurus* may have been nearly a full foot longer than *T. rex's*. Yet *T. rex* had a much broader skull and stronger jaw muscles. This meant that it had the far bigger bite of the two. *Giganotosaurus* had weak teeth in comparison. Although they were more adept at slicing flesh, they were more likely to shatter on contact with bone. *T. rex* also had massive eyes (larger than *Giganotosaurus*) and therefore very keen eyesight. *T. rex* almost certainly had a better depth perception than *Giganotosaurus*. The discovery of *Giganotosaurus* cleared up a long-standing mystery; namely why *T. rex* never migrated into South America. Both of these dinosaurs occupied the same position at the top of the food chain and it now appears that *Giganotosaurus* (or maybe its descendants) kept *T. rex* out of South America. In turn, *T. rex* kept *Giganotosaurus* out of North America. The discovery of *Giganotosaurus* displaced *T. rex* as the largest predatory dinosaur. This was based on comparing the newly discovered *Giganotosaurus* with 'Sue' the largest most complete *T. rex* at the time. However, the discovery of a *T. rex* in Montana during 1997 seems set to rewrite the record books. Yet to be fully excavated and described, this *T. rex* appears to be nearly complete. Its pubis bone is at least 52 inches long (compared to 48 inches for Sue). The skull appears to be approximately two metres long. The claims of *Giganotosaurus* as the largest carnivorous dinosaur appear to have been eclipsed. Furthermore, an expedition in the summer of 2000 headed by Dr John Horner found five new *T. rexes*. Although the specimens are yet to be fully excavated, one of these is claimed to be at least ten per cent larger than Sue.

Hold the front page! Coming out of the same bone beds as the original *Giganotosaurus* discovery appear to be yet more large meat-eaters. Again, these new discoveries have yet to be properly documented but it is rumoured that they are either a larger *Giganotosaurus* or a new species of predator larger than *Giganotosaurus*. Also, a large *Spinosaurus* skull rumoured to be eight feet long has allegedly turned up recently. If that measurement was indeed correct, it would suggest that *Spinosaurus* has a legitimate claim to be the longest ever carnivorous dinosaur, but would probably not have been as heavy as either *T. rex* or *Giganotosaurus*.

So who *is* the size king?

Until these new discoveries are properly documented it is impossible to tell. No doubt this is only the beginning. With new dinosaurs discovered every week, new claimants to the carnivorous crown will no doubt keep coming forward. These creatures led very violent lives and very few would have died of old age. Most skeletons of large theropods show a violent history. The recent *Carcharodontosaurus* skeleton exhibited a puncture wound just above the nose, suggesting that they attacked each other. Sue the *T. rex*, appeared to have died violently, having one side of her face ripped off. The wounds seem to correspond with those of another *T. rex*, more than likely a larger specimen. Tantalisingly there is also the possibility that the attack came from a larger but different type of as yet undiscovered theropod. We cannot speculate on the future; we can only go on what we currently have available. If I were a betting man my money would remain on *T. rex*. *T. rex* may have briefly lost the size crown in the 1990s but appears set to regain it. It is the boxing equivalent of losing your title after a long reign, but then immediately regaining it in your next fight.

Anyway, even if *Giganotosaurus* had a size advantage, when push comes to shove *T. rex* bites much harder and penetrates more deeply than any dinosaur yet discovered. It was correctly named in 1904 – the tyrant lizard king. Still, no predatory dinosaur yet discovered can challenge the current incumbent for the title of 'heaviest terrestrial predator of all time'. That title belongs to the ancient crocodilians....

Predator Deathmatch

TYRANNOSAURUS REX IN PROFILE

Length   40 feet +

Weight   7 tonnes +

Weaponry   6-inch-long teeth, housed in a robust jaw made for bone crushing

Speed   Up to 20mph

Weaknesses   What weaknesses?

Profile   The meanest carnivorous dinosaur ever to roam the earth

Human Champ   Evander Holyfield narrowly avoids the first bone-crushing bite, but is unfortunately trampled underfoot on the follow-through. He survived for 3.5 seconds.

SUPER CROC

It is widely accepted amongst palaeontologists that the largest predator that walked on land was not a dinosaur. Instead it was a crocodilian. Today's crocodiles and alligators are direct descendents from the time of the dinosaurs. Whereas the dinosaurs were wiped out by environmental changes, the crocodilians adapted and continue to flourish to this very day. Indeed, they still exist as apex predators at the top of the food chain. A large saltwater crocodile today can exceed twenty feet in length and weigh over a tonne. Today crocs are responsible for hundreds of human deaths every year. They are capable of killing very large prey and Nile crocodiles have been observed taking unwary lions. As impressive as today's crocodiles are in the predatory stakes, they are mere babies when compared to their prehistoric relatives.

One of the largest – perhaps *the* largest – of these crocodilians was called *Deinosuchus*. To the casual observer it would appear to be a cross between an oversized crocodile and an oversized alligator. On closer scrutiny subtle differences between *Deinosuchus* and modern crocodilians become apparent; e.g. the teeth are very thick and unusually blunt in the middle and rear jaws.

Most of the knowledge of *Deinosuchus* comes from skulls, jaws and miscellaneous bones from behind the skull. Well preserved remains that represent a substantial part of the body are unfortunately still lacking. Thus here again begins much of the detective work in piecing together what this animal actually looked like.

Historically, *Deinosuchus* has also been known as *Phobosuchus* ('fearful crocodile'), but it is

now accepted that these creatures are one and the same. Because no complete skeleton of *Deinosuchus* has ever been found, in order to calculate the size, extrapolations have to be made based on comparisons with modern day alligators and crocodiles. Although not an exact science, this does nevertheless provide us with a useful reference. The larger specimens of *Deinosuchus* had skulls exceeding two metres in length. A 1954 paper by Colbert and Bird estimated the length of *Deinosuchus* at over 50 feet on the basis of skull fragments from an individual specimen. This has frequently been repeated as the size of *Deinosuchus* in both popular books and more sophisticated paleontological literature. Indeed, on the basis of such an analysis, some scientists have postulated that large individuals could weigh anything up to eighteen tonnes, over twice the weight of an adult *Tyrannosaurus rex*.

However, more modern analyses of *Deinosuchus* remains suggest, in fact, that the 1954 analysis over-estimated the size of the fearful crocodile. A more careful study of the available material has been conducted by David Schwimmer (not the bloke from *Friends*!). It would appear that there were two different populations of *Deinosuchus*: one that lived on the eastern coast of the United States and a larger cousin that lived on the western coast. Schwimmer puts the overall body length of the eastern species at around twenty-seven feet, a little larger than today's largest saltwater crocodiles. However, the western species grew considerably larger, giving a large *Deinosuchus* a total body length of approximately 40 feet.

Using similar extrapolations it is possible to estimate body weights for these large crocodilians. Here the numbers become quite amazing. Crocodilians are well known to increase their mass exponentially with increased length. Weights are rarely recorded for modern day crocodiles because of the obvious difficulties in doing so. However, it is estimated that a twenty-foot Nile crocodile will exceed one tonne. Various formulas have been developed to estimate the weights of large specimens but the different formulas produce wildly differing results. A study of small captive alligators dating from 1973 (Thomas Coulson et al) produced a formula linking total length to body weight. However, the largest animal in this study barely exceeded six feet. The authors of the study made a cautionary note about extrapolating the weight of animals exceeding ten feet. Nevertheless, given their formula, a 40-foot *Deinosuchus* produces a weight of 16.4 metric tonnes.

A more recent study was conducted in 1989 by Webb and Manolis. This was based on extrapolations from measurements of captive saltwater crocodiles. Using their estimates a typical twenty-seven-foot eastern specimen would weigh in at around 2.3 tonnes. Webb and Manolis only extrapolate for specimens up to 33 feet in length. However, Schwimmer has further extrapolated their extrapolations and this provides us with a 40-foot *Deinosuchus* weighing in at around 8.5 tonnes.

Clearly, estimating the weight of *Deinosuchus* from such basic, fragmentary data lacks both precision and accuracy. However, of the two studies the latter provides us with a more accurate estimation. The data was extracted based on measurements from today's largest crocodile and therefore has more relevance to *Deinosuchus* than six-foot alligators. Also, it is hard to imagine a sixteen-tonne crocodile being even remotely mobile out of the water. At forty feet in length a bodyweight of sixteen tonnes simply seems too excessive. By contrast, the 8.5 tonne estimate is far from excessive. Indeed, it is probably conservative. Therefore, to summarize these calculations, *T. rex* is likely to find himself outweighed. At 8.5 tonnes, a large *Deinosuchus* is still 1.5 tonnes heavier than the estimated weight for a large *T. rex* (possibly except the 1997 Montana find), traditionally the giant carnivore benchmark.

Deinosuchus was probably the apex predator of its time. It was sufficiently large enough to kill most contemporary late Cretaceous nearshore and marine life. Exceptions to this may have included the larger mososaurs and pliosaurs (see next chapter). *Deinosuchus* (both eastern and western types) were equal or larger than any known land predators of their age. Their main rivals for Daddy status at the time were medium-sized tyrannosaurids such as *Albertosaurus* (up to 10m in length). *T. rex* himself did not evolve until *Deinosuchus* became extinct.

Given that a gigantic crocodilian lived at the same time as large meat-eating dinosaurs, natural questions arise about who was eating what and whom. The very first description of *Deinosuchus* made explicit speculation about it having evolved its great size to prey on dinosaurs. Indeed, this 1954 description gave a list of possible *Deinosuchus* food, including hadrosaurs, ceratopsians, sauropods and ankylosaurs. When scientists attempt to recreate the feeding behaviours of extinct animals they start by assuming that the extinct animals behaved similarly to their living relatives. *Deinosuchus*, as a huge crocodilian, was an apex predator capable of feeding on large prey, with some victims approaching or even exceeding its own size. Modern crocodilians feed on a wide variety of species dependent on circumstance and environment.

The most direct evidence of any prey selection in an extinct species is to find fossil remains of the stomach contents. Similarly, predation can be analysed further down the digestive system with the study of preserved faeces (coprolites), searching for undigested, identifiable bits of the prey within the faeces. However, to date neither of these methods has shed any light on *Deionosuchus's* diet. Firstly, the remains of *Deinosuchus* so far discovered have been fragmentary; no specimen has divulged stomach contents! Secondly, although some coprolites have been discovered that could be attributable to *Deinosuchus,* this is not conclusive. Furthermore, none of the bits of bone in the said coprolites are identifiable.

However, there is other evidence of *Deinosuchus* predation. The smaller eastern deinosuchids may have fed largely on sea turtles. Modern alligators certainly prey frequently on freshwater turtles. A large, now extinct, sea turtle called *Bothremys* has revealed predatory bite marks on its remains that appear to be crocodilian in origin. Furthermore, some fossilised *Deinosuchus* teeth show signs of having bitten some very hard surfaces (turtle shells perhaps). Although there is some degree of assumption in this predator-prey nexus it is a fairly logical one. More interestingly there is now some explicit evidence that the eastern deinosuchids were preying on dinosaurs. It is obvious that deinosuchids were large enough to kill and eat at least some dinosaurs. Yet it is unknown whether their large sizes were achieved because dinosaurs were abundant as potential food or whether, by virtue of their large size, this allowed them to prey on dinosaurs.

One of the most distinctive features of *Deinosuchus* is the heavy teeth and strong jaws. Agents of extraordinary crushing power, this allowed the disablement of small to medium-sized dinosaurs. They would have been able to paralyse sizeable dinosaurs with bites across the neck, back and pelvis. They could also crush the lower legs of bipedal dinosaurs wading through marshes, bringing them into better reach of the low slung crocodilians. Schwimmer speculates that the smaller eastern *Deinosuchus* evolved first and eventually expanded its range to the western side of the United States. The founder population encountered a habitat with a much higher, more diverse dinosaur population to that of the east. Once a viable *Deinosuchus* population had been established in the west, the enhanced opportunity for feeding on abundant and large dinosaurs would have caused a natural selection process producing increasingly larger individuals of *Deinosuchus*.

There is certainly some evidence of dinosaur predation by western deinosuchids and not only of herbivores. A paper published in 1993 (Gallagher) made brief mention of carnivorous-dinosaur teeth from a marine deposit in New Jersey that had apparently had their enamel surfaces partially dissolved away. Gallagher assumed that the enamel had been stripped away in the digestive juices of a crocodilian. *Deinosuchus* was present in the same locality and because of its size and tooth morphology we must assume that if a crocodilian was feeding on a theropod dinosaur, it would more than likely be a *Deinosuchus*. It may seem odd that *Deinosuchus* would prey on a carnivore when there were surely easier options. However, there is no reason why one carnivore would not prey in an opportunistic manner on another and evidence does exist to support the notion. Nile crocodiles have been observed preying on lions, for example. Even a large eastern *Deinosuchus* would be capable of killing a one-tonne theropod. Despite this evidence, it cannot be proved that in this instance the digested carnivore teeth are a result of *Deinosuchus* predation. Instead, it could have been a result of *Deinosuchus* scavenging on dead remains.

Still, there is further evidence of theropod predation. Schwimmer, in his studies of the southeastern coastal plains, notes that the larger carnivorous dinosaurs are absent from the fossil record, implying that some other animal occupied the top predatory role. Also, there exists a single theropod bone from the western United States that appears to have been chewed by a crocodile. The bone, thought to be a tibia, has been mutilated and has been clearly deformed from crushing. The bite marks are blunt, suggesting a crocodilian origin (as opposed to serrated bite marks from other theropods). This bone was almost certainly the result of a *Deinosuchus* killing (or scavenging) a small theropod. From the size of the bone fragment it is clear that the animal was immature and probably weighed no more than 400kg.

Certainly, an adult *Deinosuchus* could have made a quick meal out of a baby theropod. However, *Deinosuchus* never actually met his arch nemesis, Mr Rex, as they lived at different times. Indeed, even the largest theropods that lived at the same time as *Deinosuchus* were considerably smaller than the king of the crocs. The fossil record would appear to suggest that *Deinosuchus* pushed therapods away from the coastal areas, preventing them from maintaining a successful breeding population. The killer croc was undoubtedly the Daddy of his day.

There is direct evidence that the larger western species of *Deinosuchus* fed directly on large herbivorous dinosaurs. *Deinosuchus* feeding traces have been discovered on hadrosaur (bipedal duck-billed dinosaurs) bones. Schwimmer has observed many hadrosaur bones with bite marks attributable to *Deinosuchus* and he noted that there was no evidence of cracking around the margin of the bites. This suggests that the bone was fresh and wet at the time it was chewed. That is, the hadrosaur victim was likely to have been predated rather than scavenged. *Deinosuchus* has impressive credentials as a possible Rex-eater, but we may be being a little premature. There were at least two other big crocs that could rival *Deinosuchus* in size.

The first of these was *Sarcosuchus imperator*. This was recently discovered by Paul Sereno, who also re-discovered *Carcharodontosaurus*. This nightmare of prehistoric nature hails from Niger in Africa sometime around the mid-cretaceous period. Sereno hypothesised that *Sarcosuchus* lived a life similar to today's river-dwelling crocodiles (as opposed to *Deinosuchus's* coastal habitat) and estimated the length of the larger individuals at 40 feet and eight tonnes. Although rivalling *Deinosuchus* in size, *Sarcosuchus* was a narrow-snouted crocodilian, most probably closely related to today's gharial crocodilians of Asia. Gharials have very long, slender jaws and rather than bring down large prey, they predate mainly on fish. *Sarcosuchus* was more than likely an eater of *large* fish and although it may have predated on some smaller dinosaurs it would probably have lacked the weaponry to kill very large prey. Damage to its slender jaws would have risked death by starvation and it is difficult to see it being a threat to an adult Rex. *Deinosuchus* therefore retains his crocodilian crown. However, our second contender may cause *Deinosuchus* more problems. *Purussaurus brasilicus* was a Miocene caiman from the Amazon basin in Peru and Brazil. Although we have been aware of the genus for more than 100 years, recent specimens, including the reconstruction of a well preserved skull, show these alligatoroids to be broad headed with two-metre-long skulls. Estimated total body lengths exceed 40 feet and estimated weights exceed ten tonnes. A jaw fragment from the same genus has been found that extrapolates to an even larger individual than the two-metre skull, with a total body length estimated at over 45 feet. *Purussaurus* matches *Deinosuchus* for skull size and probably exceeds its bulk. So was the king of the crocs actually an alligator?

This is obviously an extremely difficult question for us to answer given that neither specimen has ever been seen alive and we can only guess their predatory behaviour and bodily dimensions from bone fragments. *Purussaurus*, living around eighteen million years ago, likely gained its huge size to prey on the large mammals of its time and probably only had to fear others of its own kind. That is, it had no natural predators. *Deinosuchus* had far greater competition for prey when it lived. Similar to the Lion vs. Tiger debate, *Deinosuchus* was probably more of a fighter as opposed to *Purussaurus* being more of a predator. However, we cannot be sure of this. Similar to lions fighting off other lions to rule the pride, adult *Purussaurus* could have fought each other to be the dominant crocodilian.

It is an extremely difficult one to call. *Purussaurus* may have slightly outweighed *Deinosuchus,* but this is arguably attributable to *Deinosuchus* being more 'in shape at the weight'. That is *Deinosuchus* had more competition for prey and was in fighting condition as opposed to *Purussaurus* carrying a few too many extra pounds from all that herbivorous consumption. Given that *Deinosuchus* was more familiar with tackling dinosaurs head on, it will therefore go forward to represent the crocs in the all-consuming showdown to find the Daddy of the prehistoric land gods!

DEINOSUCHUS IN PROFILE

Length	40 feet +
Weight	8.5 tonnes +
Weaponry	A mouth full of blunt 5 inch bone-crushing spikes.
Speed	Very explosive in short bursts, probably in excess of 20mph
Weaknesses	Really?
Profile	The Dinosaur Killer
Human Champ	Evander Holyfield approaches cautiously and is ignored by the croc king who looks like he is ready for bed. Holyfield unleashes his best shots into the armour plating of the 40 foot beast (you have to admire his persistence). Unperturbed, the croc darts forward with lightning speed, crushing Holyfield in an instant before swallowing him almost whole. He lasted 14.6 seconds.

BIG FIGHT BUILD UP

Well, here we have it at last; the battle of the biggest, nastiest killers ever to roam the earth. You wouldn't want to meet either of these critters in a dark alley. In fact you couldn't because they wouldn't fit into the alley!

There have been lots of negotiations prior to the securing of this bout. The *Deinosuchus* Camp wanted it held in five feet of surf shoreline with the option of retreating to deeper waters. The *T. rex* camp flatly refused, protesting that this was to establish the king of the land killers and that any bout should be held at least ten miles inshore. A compromise was reached when it was finally agreed that the bout would be held on a dry sandy shore backing onto a shallow lagoon no more than six feet in depth. It is unclear how the conditions will help/hinder the antagonists.

A lot of the smart money is going on the croc king. Many of the experts feel that he just needs to secure a grip on the *T. rex* leg and drag him into the abyss. However, key questions remain over the performance of the croc king and his ability to perform his killer move. The crux of these doubts hovers over the previous fight record of the super croc. He may be used to bringing down large dinosaurs (including medium sized theropods), but he has simply never faced anything like the Tyrant Lizard King. Bringing down a juvenile *Albertosaurus* is nothing like tackling a bull *Tyrannosaurus rex*. Even bringing down relatively large herbivores cannot compare; they simply do not have the weaponry to launch a counter-assault. Mr Rex represents the King Croc's worst nightmare with extra helpings.

The Rex has got that bone-crushing bite that is capable of tearing chunks out of the super croc. Super croc may have the bite pressure but he simply can't tear off flesh in the same way. He will have to rely on the bite and drag followed by the death roll. Also, many observers have pointed out that *Deinosuchus* will not have the reliance of his learned friends and colleagues for this match up. This is no tag match. If he successfully drags *T. rex* into the deeper waters, no fellow crocs are going to pounce and help him finish the job. He's all alone out there.

A further bone of contention is the height issue and how this plays into the hands of either combatant. Some are saying that the super-croc has a major problem due to its diminutive, squat stature. How can it hit what it can't reach? Others, however, are saying this unusual feature represents a distinct advantage. Mr Rex will have to stoop down to attack his rather large adversary, something he is not used to doing and something that may limit his effectiveness. Super croc, however, is used to this predicament. He is used to employing smash, grab and drag tactics. He regularly grabs a leg and drags his prey into deep waters. Many of his prey items have been tall bipedal dinosaurs; that is, *T. rex*-shaped, just not as large. The key question on everybody's lips is whether super croc can effectively handle the extra tonnage in his prospective prey.

Both will be wary of each other. Neither has experience of such a dangerous adversary. Expect a chess match early on....

SECONDS OUT

The tension was evident between the combatants as they entered the arena. The Super Croc immediately took residence in the shallow water, whilst the Tyrant Lizard King slinked his way around the outside of the sandy perimeter edge, not taking his great big eyes of the Super Croc. There was something of a tense stand-off as the two super critters eyeballed each other with malicious intent. After approximately two minutes of atmosphere that was so tense it nearly melted around us, the Super Croc began to emit what is best described as a low guttural, hissing sound. The Dino-King let out an almighty roar in response, prompting a swift lunge in reply with those gaping jaws from the Super Croc. However, the attempted leg-grab was only half-hearted and served more as a warning. Another more serious attempted leg-grab ensued, but the Super Croc was out of range when the Rex simply stepped back. *T. rex* attempted nothing in response to these gestures of aggression, perhaps daunted by the short, squat musculature of his unusual adversary.

Suddenly, with a deafening roar and whoosh of spray, the Super Croc exploded from his crouched position, making a serious lunge at his bipedal opponent. *T. rex* was caught unawares, and although reacting by stepping back, those six-foot jaws got a slender/moderate hold on the right leg of the Tyrant Lizard King. The super croc began to instinctively drag *T. rex* towards the water, attempting to use his weight advantage to its full effect. The lower foreleg of the *T. rex* was partially crushed by the closing force of the vice-like jaws, but that was far from the end of the contest. As if an alarm bell had suddenly sounded within the *T. rex,* driven on by a combination of fear, hunger and sheer will to survive, he bent down and took a chunk clean out of the upper back of the *Deinosuchus*. The super croc instantly let go of his hold on the leg and retreated to his watery den in obvious distress. The *Deinosuchus* bite may have crushed the foreleg bone like an industrial car crusher squeezes the last bits of life out of Jaguar (not the feline kind) but the *T. rex* bite did more damage. It did far more than crush bone. It tore clean through the armour plating on the back of the croc and ripped away muscle, sinew and bone, all in one foul movement.

Both combatants were injured but perhaps sensing a victory, the *T. rex* hobbled after its equally damaged opponent. The Super Croc again lunged at the Rex, again half-heartedly, warning the giant carnivore to stay away. The Rex was in no position to use footwork, but the Super Croc was also on the ropes, bleeding profusely from its wound. The Rex was not to be deterred and he lumbered on into the shallow waters. The Super Croc opened its mouth wide, revealing its huge gape. Yet this seemed little more than a warning now. Crucially, the tide of this battle had turned. Being cold-blooded the super croc had used most of its energy stores with those few explosive lunges. Ideally, it now needed to retreat to a solarium to recover. *T. rex* suffered from no such defect. The Super Croc continued to open its mouth wide whilst emitting a low pitched grunting noise in an attempt to scare the Rex away. But the tyrant lizard was starving and pressed forth its attack. A well timed lunge saw the Dino-King take a significant piece out of the side wall of the skull of the super croc. *T. rex* retreated to chew on the bone, sinew and tissue from its latest successful attack. *Deinosuchus* thrashed about in confusion and pain. It was the start of its death throes. The next attack from the Tyrant Lizard would prove fatal to the super croc. *Tyrannosaurus rex* confirmed his position as the ultimate predator ever to have walked the earth.

POST-MATCH ANALYSIS

Whilst the tyrant lizard emerged triumphant from this clash the debate raged amongst those at ringside on whether he could reproduce his performance in the event of a re-match. After all, *T. rex* was critically injured by the leg-grab manoeuvre and some are saying he was lucky to produce his counter-attack when he did. Obviously given the extinct nature of the two combatants we have to make a large number of assumptions and guesswork to fill in the many gaps that their fossilised remains do not answer. We cannot watch tapes of their predatory behaviour like we can with today's ultimate killers. The scientists often interpret things differently and some of their theories are wrong and open to re-shaping over time.

It would appear a reasonable assumption that *Deinosuchus* had many biological and behavioural similarities with modern crocodiles. The crucial biological simile drawn out in our particular clash was the fact that *Deinosuchus* was a cold-blooded reptile, the same as all modern day crocodilians. This means that the super croc was only able to sustain a few attacks before its muscles became filled with lactic acid and it needed to rest for a sustained period. This left it open and susceptible to attack from its deadly rival.

Unfortunately for the analysts in this match-up *T. rex* has no close modern day relative. Indeed, the birds in our gardens may well be some of the Tyrant Lizard's closing living relatives and it goes without saying that they hardly instil fear into us when they descend from the sky. So much of what we know about *T. rex* comes from calculated guesswork and so much of what we know is heavily disputed by different groups of palaeontologists. Some argue vehemently that *T. rex* was only a scavenger that mugged smaller predators for their kills. Others argue that it was the ultimate predator, hunting down very large prey. Some state that *T. rex* was a fast runner that could burst from the undergrowth and ambush an unwary herbivore with stealth and surprise. The rival camp suggests that a fall from a sprinting *T. rex* could result in death for the Tyrant Lizard King (crushed under its own body weight) and therefore it would be unable to run at any great speed.

Traditionally it has long been assumed that all dinosaurs were cold-blooded. However, recent evidence in the study of *T. rex* has suggested that this long held belief may well be erroneous. Analysis of *T. rex* bones shows evidence of the animal in fact being warm-blooded. However, the evidence is far from conclusive either way and the crux of this battle may well indeed rest on this fact. It is hard to make a strong case for *Deinosuchus* if we assume it has this handicap. It would have to strike early and conclusively to bring down the *Tyrannosaurus*. If the battle became prolonged the balance of power would naturally shift to the warm-blooded predator. If, however, both combatants were cold-blooded, the battle evens somewhat with any endurance advantage being removed.

At the end of the day, we have very little supportive evidence to guide us in this clash of the titans. The super croc may well have had the superior bulk, but its weaponry seems a little inferior when put alongside the Daddy dinosaur. If I had to put my house on it, I'd still back a cold-blooded *Tyrannosaurus rex* to triumph on most occasions.

HOLD THE FRONT PAGE

In the wake of defeat, more bad news is being piled onto *Deinosuchus*. There are palaeontological whisperings afoot! Although not yet widely known or discussed (as of November 2009), some palaeontologists are claiming that everything we have claimed for *Deinosuchus* is wrong.

The picture on page 55 shows a museum specimen of a *Deinosuchus* skull, which had been constructed from a very limited number of bone fragments and scaled up according to modern crocodilian proportions. However, new theories are suggesting that this was in error and *Deinosuchus* may have been more like a gigantic gharial crocodile, with a long narrow snout specialised for catching fish.

This would mean *Deinosuchus* was more closely related to *Sarcosuchus* whose claims to be the Supercroc were rejected because of his fish eating habits. It is highly unlikely that a gharial type prehistoric crocodile could predate on large dinosaurs. That long narrow snout would simply be too vulnerable and unsuited for bringing down large prey.

Of course, the *Deinosuchus* camp flatly deny the new claims of these 'pesky palaeontologists', claiming the croc king is still exactly that. They are hurriedly gathering bone experts to their cause to challenge the claims of these new bone experts. If only these scientific types could make up their minds!

However, *Purassaurus*, that 45-foot Miocene caiman is now staking his claim to be the Supercroc more strongly than ever. *T Rex* might have a new legitimate contender to the throne…….

Chapter 4
Aquatic Battle of the Ages
Megalodon vs. Megapli

GREAT TOOTH

Having seen our combatants battle for supremacy on the land throughout the annals of time, now the tide turns and we head back into the sea. The cogs of our time machine whir into action again, for as formidable as our modern day oceanic predators are, they would be nothing more than fish food for some of the predators that roamed our oceans in prehistoric times.

The first of our contenders in this battle of the water-breathers is truly a creature from our worst nightmares. When Peter Benchley first began to formulate the story behind the book *Jaws*, he was struck with a dilemma. At first he couldn't decide whether to write a book about a seaside town being terrorised by a great white shark or whether to write a book about a prehistoric leviathan eating swimmers, boats or anything else that happened to stray into its path. That leviathan would have been our first contender - *Carcharodon megalodon*.

Megalodon (which translated means 'great tooth') first appeared in the world's oceans approximately sixteen million years ago, during the Miocene period. There is some evidence that it may have emerged much earlier – about 50 million years ago – but the evidence has been poorly documented or is believed to be the result of misidentification on the part of certain researchers.

I first became aware of this monster shark (you guessed it) as a young child trawling through my trusty *Guinness Book of Records*. There was an astonishing photograph of several men in white coats standing in what looked like the mouth of an enormous great white shark. These men were indeed standing upright! The attached blurb told of a giant shark that roamed the prehistoric seas and was related to the modern day *Carcharodon carcharias* (great white). This thing made the great white look like a guppy in comparison! Based on fossilised teeth, scientists had estimated the length of this nightmarish predator at around 80 feet.

Sharks have a cartilaginous skeleton that does not readily fossilise. Most species of ancient shark are known from their teeth only, which are much more durable structures. Megalodon is no exception to this general rule.

In subsequent editions of the *Guinness Book of Records*, I was disappointed to note that the size of megalodon began to shrink. Apparently the 80ft estimate was based on an incorrect reconstruction of the shark's jaws, with certain teeth being placed at inappropriate spots in the mouth. A revised estimate gave a surprisingly precise 43 feet as the total body length. In one edition of the record book I distinctly remember it giving this revised length and then adding that this was comparable with the largest great whites that roam the oceans today! This is of course palpable nonsense and as has been demonstrated in previous chapters we must take with a pinch of salt anything that is stated in the *Guinness Book of Records*, particularly from older editions. This claim is made to seem even more ridiculous when we compare the teeth of the two monster sharks. Great white and megalodon teeth bear a striking resemblance in shape; they are both triangular with serrated edges. However, great white teeth rarely exceed two inches in total length. Megalodon teeth have been known to reach seven inches (and are obviously much bulkier). This puts into perspective the relative sizes of the two sharks and anyone who suggests that even the largest of white sharks is comparable is surely away with the tooth fairies!

Indeed, the similarity in the shape of the teeth between modern white sharks and megalodons led many researchers to envisage megalodon as simply a much larger and bulkier version of the white shark. Traditionally it was assumed that megalodon was an ancestor to the white shark, whereas recent research suggests that it was in fact only a close relative. To get technical for a moment, there is a fair degree of controversy of the phylogeny of megalodon. Those who think it is related to the white shark believe that it should be placed in the genus *Carcharodon*. Others subscribe to the theory that it is only a distant relative of Jaws and that it should be given its own genus – *Carcharocles*. This would place it is a separate lineage that eventually gave way to modern day sand tiger sharks. If this latter theory is true, then megalodon may not have looked much like a white shark at all, but possibly like an oversized sand tiger shark with a much broader head (than the white shark). Those that subscribe to this theory also argue that given its size, megalodon would have to be like an oversized sand tiger, as an oversized white shark would simply be too bulky and heavy to be effective (sand tigers are far more streamlined than great whites). I do not intend to get into the somewhat technical *Carcharodon* vs. *Carcharocles* debate here. For the sake of argument we shall just refer to our contender as megalodon.

There is some debate as to when megalodon actually died out and ceased to become a threat to other ocean inhabitants. The general consensus is that megalodon died out about 1.5 million years ago. However, there is some evidence that megalodon actually survived much later than that. A pair of five-inch megalodon teeth, dredged up from a depth of 4300m in the South Pacific, was dated in 1959 as being between 11,000 and 24,000 years old. Such a period is a mere blink of the eye in geological time and may have meant that our ancient ancestors actually could have formed part of the megalodon diet if they ventured into the water!

Indeed, despite the general consensus among zoologists and palaeontologists that megalodon is no more, it has been suggested by many cryptozoologists and other researchers that this enormous shark may actually continue to exist in the deep sea or other part of the ocean. Such proponents cite a small body of evidence for their claims including only recently fossilised teeth and eyewitness accounts. One such account was recounted by the Australian naturalist David Stead. In 1918 he recorded the sensation among the crayfishermen at Port Stephens when for several days they refused to go to their regular fishing grounds in the vicinity of Broughton Island. The men had been at work on the fishing grounds when an immense shark of almost unbelievable proportions put in an appearance, lifting pot after pot containing many crashfish and taking, as the men said, "pots, mooring lines and all". These crayfish pots were each about three-foot-six in diameter and contained approximately thirty crayfish, each weighing several pounds. The men were all unanimous that the shark was something the like of which they had never even dreamed! Stead said that the lengths they gave were absurd. One said it was as long as the wharf on which they stood (115 feet). They were all familiar with whales, which they had often seen passing but this, they all agreed, was a vast shark. Stead described them as prosaic and stolid men, not given to 'fish' stories. One of the things that impressed Stead was that they all agreed as to the ghostly whitish colour of the vast fish. He concluded that it must have been something really gigantic to have put such experienced men into a state of panic.

Although it is not our intention here to discuss the veracity of megalodon survival in detail, one more tale makes interesting reading; that is the story of the Australian cutter *Rachel Cohen*. Whilst in an Adelaide dry dock in 1954, workers found seventeen teeth embedded in the ship's wooden hull that reportedly resembled those of the white shark. However, they were unusually large for a white shark, being over four inches in length. The teeth were arranged in a semi-circle (typical of a shark bite), about six feet in diameter and the bite, if that's what it was, was near the propeller. The propeller shaft had been bent. The *Rachel Cohen*'s captain recalled a shudder to the boat experienced one night during a storm near Timor in Indonesia. He had assumed that the boat had collided with a floating tree trunk.

These are not the only tales to support megalodon survival into the present day. There are several other 'large fish stories' on record. However, it is very difficult to check the validity of such tales. Eyewitness testimony is fragile at the best of times. People often lie, exaggerate or make basic human errors. These very human flaws are often compounded further if the witness has just been scared or frightened by the appearance of a creature from the ocean depths that is not only big enough to eat them, but also to sink their boat ! It is very difficult to know what to make of such reports without being able to check the stories back to their original sources. However, as has been demonstrated in earlier chapters, tales of outsized white sharks tended to evaporate under the scrutiny of officious research. It is difficult to dismiss tales of 100ft sharks as simply exaggeration or error. Either the whole story is fallacious, has grown with several retellings or possibly, the creature was misidentified (a large whale perhaps). Tantalisingly there also exists the possibility that either a gigantic unknown shark, or a shark previously thought extinct, still roams the oceans.

To this particular writer the latter option seems unlikely. If megalodon or something like it did still exist it seems logical that we would have more evidence of its existence than a few scared fishermen and a damaged propeller. The notion that it lives in the ocean depths seems unlikely. The current paleoecological view is that megalodon inhabited tropical waters and like the extant white shark, was a coastal species. In order for it to have been a deep-sea inhabitant, it would have had to prey largely on giant squid (see next chapter). It seems unlikely that a creature as large and adapted to a coastal, warm and food-rich marine habitat as megalodon could survive in the cold, food-poor deep sea.

For the purposes of this chapter we will assume that megalodon is extinct. This enables the orca and the white shark to have their battle unopposed. Otherwise we would have to assume that they would both end up as lunch. Megalodon has a far larger problem on its hands and had larger prey to hunt. So what did megalodon eat?

As has already been mentioned, it seems unlikely that megalodon was a deep-sea inhabitant. Another of our later contenders, the giant squid, could therefore rest easy. Millions of years of evolution would instead have moulded megalodon into an active, shallow-water predator, as opposed to a squid-eating leviathan. Early baleen whales and large pinnipeds were both likely food sources, as also were sea crocodiles, sea turtles and other sharks. Megalodons probably fed on much the same prey items as today's large predatory sharks. The crucial difference between a megalodon and a great white, for example, is that megalodon could take much larger prey. There were very few things in the ocean large enough not to fear megalodon. Indeed, as the white shark and megalodon co-existed for several million years, the white shark was probably a prey item in the prehistoric seas and was not, as it is today, an apex predator. Today's hunter was yesterday's lunch.

In a similar fashion to modern day sharks, megalodon is likely to have scavenged when it could. Whale meat was likely to have been a preferred delicacy. However, megalodon didn't wait for a whale to die and decompose, thereby providing an easy meal. He actively went out to hunt whales and didn't need a harpoon! We know that the giant ancestral shark fed on whales because their remains have often been found together, with the whale bones bearing all the hallmarks of megalodon teeth. Indeed, one particular investigation of the remains of a 30 ft baleen whale shows megalodon to be a chillingly efficient killer. Gashes made by the six-inch teeth revealed how megalodon snapped onto its hapless victim, crushing vital organs. Many of the whale bones showing predation from megalodon exhibit bite marks around the shoulder region, which is considered unusual. This shows a distinct difference between the attack mechanisms of the modern white shark and megalodon. Great white teeth are delicate and break away easily. White sharks bite their prey then often spit it out again, circling whilst the prey item bleeds to death, before moving in to feed. This smash-and-ambush tactic protects the shark's teeth and indeed the shark itself from damage caused by a thrashing victim desperate to live. The white will often launch a surprise attack from below with the victim knowing nothing of the danger until it is too late. Megalodon teeth, however, were much thicker and stronger (even accounting for the relative size difference). Many megalodon teeth have been found that have had their tips snapped off at the end, suggesting that the shark bit onto the shoulder of the hapless whale and held on as it struggled in its death throes. If the white shark can be compared to a light-on-his-feet stick-and-move boxer, megalodon is more a bar room brawler.

We need to know, however, how large the biggest megalodon prey was. In short, we don't really know. Much would depend on the size of the individual shark. So the question becomes how *big* did megalodon grow? Due to a complete lack of skeletal fossil finds, again nobody can be sure. We can only extrapolate our best guesses from its teeth. We know now that the famous picture of the reconstructed megalodon jaws containing six scientists, some of them standing upright, was completely inaccurate. Despite this the jaws remain on display in the American Museum of Natural History in New York today. Indeed, a label accompanies these immense jaws, prepared in 1940, in which it states that with jaws nine feet across, the shark probably reached an approximate length of 45 feet. If we accepted those jaws to be of accurate reconstruction, it would be fairly obvious that their owner must have been considerably larger than 45 feet! It doesn't take a genius to realise that someone made a mistake in either the reconstruction or the estimated length. Some observers have simply assumed that the length estimate was in error. In his book *Shark Safari*, Hal Scharp postulates a length of 120 feet for megalodon. If we accepted the jaws as nine feet across, this 'guesstimate' would not be too far wrong! Also, a few other authors have conveniently assumed the same thing. Robin Brown wrote a fictional book called *Megalodon* with 200-foot sharks that were eventually dispatched by a trained sperm whale! How the sperm whale avoided being lunch can only be guessed at! It is widely accepted now that those jaws are poorly reconstructed. They assumed a uniform length for all the teeth, whereas the teeth at the back of the jaws are in fact smaller in all sharks. Other megalodon jaws have been reconstructed more accurately at other institutions and are roughly half the size of the New York reconstruction.

So where does this leave us? Well, all we have to go on are the teeth. They are similar in shape to a great white tooth, but roughly three times the length. If we therefore scale everything up, the average megalodon would be approximately three times the length of an average white shark (but obviously considerably bulkier and much, much heavier). The average white shark is approximately fifteen feet in length, so using logic, the average megalodon must have been around about 45 feet. One wonders if this is where the New York exhibitors came up with their own 45 feet figure. However, as we well know, an average white shark may be around fifteen feet in length, but they do grow considerably larger. Specimens exceeding twenty feet have been caught, measured and accurately verified. Specimens still larger appear likely and twenty-five-foot white sharks probably represent the upper length of the species. Therefore, by scaling up our large white shark into a large megalodon, a great tooth in the region of 70 feet seems distinctly plausible. Certainly, most scientists who have written papers on our quarry give lengths in the region of 50-60 feet, and it seems fairly safe to assume that an outsized version could certainly exceed this.

Why megalodon, with its seven-inch teeth, vast bulk and a mouth that could accommodate an average office desk, should have disappeared remains a mystery. The most likely theory is that megalodon may have died out because of the extinction of its major food source – early baleen whales. Other possible theories exist and include possible changes in oceanic circulation, the closing of the Isthmus of Panama (which may have cut off access to mating and pupping areas) and even competition from other large predators. The latter point is of particular interest. Before we get excited, however, nobody thinks that megalodon was eaten by a larger predator. Most likely is that more successful hunters evolved and thereby deprived megalodon of it meals. The most likely candidates for this would have been orcas. As well as being chillingly efficient and even brutal hunters, orcas are also highly *intelligent* hunters. Their deployment of teamwork when hunting probably gave them a considerable advantage over the lone megalodons enabling them to snare their prey more effectively. In addition, both adult orcas and white sharks could have potentially eaten young megalodons and increased the essence of competition. Also, the whales that survived and evolved into the species we know today may simply have been too fast for megalodon to catch. These new whales also showed a trend towards colder waters, to which megalodon was unsuited. In essence, a combination of factors resulted in a lessened food supply and in a strange twist of fate megalodon may have starved to death. It appears that megalodon may have evolved into smaller, faster, nimbler sharks that were better able to catch the prey items of the day.

However, Richard Ellis and John McCosker in their outstanding work *Great White Shark* sum things up as follows: "At 50 feet or more, Megalodon was probably the most terrifying predator that ever lived". Probably, but maybe not….

MEGALODON IN PROFILE

Length   50-70 feet

Weight   Up to 50 tonnes

Weaponry   Over 100, 6-inch long serrated teeth made for ripping

Speed   Up to 20mph

Weaknesses   Mobility

Profile   Solitary predator, feeding mainly on medium-sized whales, or any thing else it could catch.

Human Champ   Evander Holyfield was unlucky to be in megalodon's path and is swallowed almost whole after only 3 seconds. Only his two feet remain as they float to the bottom of the ocean.

BIG MOUTH

Cryptozoology is the study of unknown or 'hidden' animals. It is something of a fledgling science with a growing interest amongst the mainstream. Monster hunters have historically formed a large majority of its proponents and perhaps the most famous of all cryptozoological quarries has been the Loch Ness monster. One of the more popular, though unlikely, explanations for the mystery at Loch Ness is that a long-necked fish-eating reptile called *Plesiosaurus* has somehow survived the dinosaur extinction event and made its home in the loch. This popular view of Nessie has it ranging from 20-40 feet in length with a long neck and four paddles/flippers extending from its body. Despite being a fascinating topic, we are not here to discuss the validity, or otherwise, of Nessie and her cousins.

Nessie is often painted as a gentle giant, and *Plesiosaurus* may well have been so. Its long neck would have meant it certainly wasn't very effective at consuming large prey. It was made for catching and eating fish. However, *Plesiosaurus* had a much shorter-necked cousin. The short-necked pliosaur was a much more formidable predator and there is some debate as to who the largest and most ferocious of these creatures was.

As a child my fascination with dinosaurs and other prehistoric reptiles and my numerous books on the subject meant that I was familiar with a creature that was discovered in Australia and went under the name of *Kronosaurus*. Indeed, the 1989 *Guinness Book of Records* states:

'the largest marine reptile ever recorded was Kronosaurus queenslandicus, *a short necked pliosuar from the Early Cretaceous (about 135 million years ago) of Australia. It had a 10ft long skull containing 80 massive teeth and measured up to 50 feet in length.'*

The 1994 *Guinness Book of Records* contained the same information, but by the time of the 1999 edition they had ceased to report on such interesting animal facts and preferred to list cat aerobics. Needless to say, I haven't bought another edition since.

Actually, the largest mounted specimen of *Kronosuarus* is 42 feet long, but it is probably safe to assume that larger individuals existed. This would have put it into a similar size bracket to the revised megalodon figure also cited in the *Guinness Book*.

As we entered the new millennium the BBC broadcast a new series upon which they had been hard at work – *Walking with Dinosaurs* (*WWD*). This was an interesting attempt at a wildlife documentary with dinosaurs represented by a mixture of models and the latest computer graphics. The voice-over then relayed to the viewer interesting dinosaur facts as though we had all the creatures on film and had been able to analyse their behaviour simply by observation. I found the programme less than entertaining, bordering on irritating because it was much more style than substance. The researchers and programme makers had made enormous leaps of faith in many areas to fill in the gaps that were not answered by the fossil record.

The third programme of the series began with a medium-sized (five-metre-long) theropod dinosaur by the waters edge. The voice-over made a veiled reference to the predator stalking its prey when suddenly the theropod was plucked from the rock on which it stood by an enormous marine predator, which carried it off to a watery grave for consumption. This action obviously caught my attention and ensured I would watch the rest of the programme!

What ensued took some believing. Their theropod-eating pliosaur was a *Liopleurodon*. *Walking with Dinosaurs* claimed that *Liopleurodon* grew up to 80 feet in length and could weigh as much as a blue whale! Furthermore, a subsequent book published under the banner of the programme rated what they considered to be the top seven oceanic predators throughout the prehistoric ages. Needless to say they rated *Liopleurodon* as *numero uno*, stating that it could pretty much eat anything in its path! Megalodon, interestingly, was only rated as the third nastiest predator in their list, being supplanted by a giant mosasaur. This was simply too much to take. Mosasaur fossils show evidence of having been preyed on by large sharks of the day, sharks considerably smaller than megalodon.

There is a definite 'gold standard' in palaeontology consisting of those animals that attract a lot of public attention. The biggest and fiercest extinct animals such as *T. rex* and *Giganotosaurus* are firmly ensconced within this section. When the BBC broadcast *Walking with Dinosaurs* they firmly stamped *Liopleurodon ferox* (to give its correct name) with the gold mark. Here was an animal that made *T. rex* look like a harmless puppy. 80 feet+ in length, with a weight of 150 tonnes; this was an awesome predator that dwarfs anything before or since.

The problem is that *Liopleurodon* (meaning 'smooth sided tooth') was not 80 feet long and did not weigh 150 tonnes. So what was *Liopleurodon*?

Liopleurodon was a large predatory marine reptile. Its remains were found throughout northern Europe and date from around 160 million years ago. It was a pliosaur and a close relative of the afore-mentioned *Kronosaurus*. The big pliosaurs were the apex predators of their day and remained so from the mid-Jurassic through to the mid-cretaceous. Unlike Nessie they have large heads and a short neck. Although they possess a similar body, it is somewhat more elongated with four paddle-like limbs. They have formidable teeth and the back of the skull is extended to make room for very large, powerful muscles, which drive the teeth into prey.

So, if the BBC got carried away, how big did *Liopleurodon* actually get in the real world? Again, to answer this question requires a large amount of speculation and educated guesswork. Identifying bones as definitely being from *Liopleurodon* is difficult and the remains of top predators are rare in general. Our knowledge of *Liopleurodon* fossils in Oxford, England has been heightened recently by the publication of a Ph.D. thesis. However, this concentrated on the skull of the creature and our knowledge of the rest of it remains limited.

The largest skull definitely belonging to *Liopleurodon* was about five feet long, but there are many ifs and buts to add. If the head was about a seventh of the overall body length (as has been the basis for many reconstructions), it would make the length of that particular specimen around 35 feet. One researcher who studied bite marks left on bones by *Liopleurodon* and then compared skull size to recognizable patterns of tooth marks, concluded that the average size for the creature was in fact only seventeen to twenty-three feet in length! He added that a larger animal would weigh in at around 2.5 tonnes. At this stage things are not looking good for our marine reptile, in fact it is looking distinctly like shark bait.

There is worse to come. The rule of the head being one seventh the length of the overall body may well be exaggerated. Many historical extrapolations have been based on the 42-foot (12.8 metre) *Kronosaurus* specimen mounted in the Harvard museum of Natural History. A substantially complete pliosuar skeleton was described in 1992 for Columbia. In this animal the head is larger in proportion to the body of the Harvard specimen and more recent work seems to confirm the same to be true of *Kronosaurus*. Therefore, the traditional models that have been used to calculate pliosaur lengths appear to have been exaggerated. A more realistic assumption is that the head was about a fifth of the overall length, not a seventh. However, despite this exaggeration in length, the bulk of the creature would have been proportionately greater.

Before we feed *Liopleurodon* and their ilk to the shark, there is some evidence of a much larger pliosaur in the Oxford clays. One such find has recently been debunked. Excitement centred on a long-neglected single vertebra, 40 per cent larger than that of *Kronosaurus*. However, upon persistent re-examination it was decided that the bone actually came from a sauropod dinosaur.

Yet other very large isolated fossils have been found, including vertebrae and large lower jaw bones. These cannot be positively identified as coming from a *Liopleurodon* and it seems equally likely that they come from an unknown species. A lower jaw reportedly in the Oxford museum collection measures ten feet in length. The author of the Ph.D. thesis believes it not to be from *Liopleurodon*. Scaling up on this basis, as with previous models, we now have an animal approaching 45-50 feet in length and considerably heavier. There have also been unconfirmed reports of a lower jaw found on the Dorset coast of England measuring thirteen feet in length, which scales the creature up to a possible length of 65 feet. Yet pliosaur mandibles are often much longer than the jaws to which they belong so caution must be exercised.

It is often said that science is not the search for truth but the search for funding. Publicity helps to secure funding and medium-sized dinosaurs and marine reptiles, no matter how interesting to researchers, simply fail to capture the public imagination.

This can often lead to a sloppy approach and a tendency to bracket the uppermost end of the size estimates as the norm. Similarly, television stations do not seek the truth; they simply seek more viewers. Their viewers represent the public imagination and it is simply more interesting to them if there is an 80-foot monster going around chewing up the sea's creatures as opposed to a 40-foot creature performing the same exercise.

However, the figures stated in *Walking with Dinosaurs* are not without basis. With a little scrutiny it is easy to see where the 80-foot figure came from. If we assume the one seventh head-body length, assume a set of ten-foot jaws based on fragmentary evidence, scale things up (70 feet) and then assume that this specimen was far from the largest one around, then voila: an 80-foot *Liopleurodon*. The weight of 150 tonnes is a little harder to understand. It is clearly based on the animal having a similar amount of bulk to a blue whale but it is hard to believe this would be the case. Furthermore, size estimates for blue whales in the region of 150 tonnes provide lengths exceeding 100 feet. An 80-foot blue whale would be considerably lighter than 150 tonnes. Furthermore, a *Liopleurodon* that weighed in at 150 tonnes would then be too slow to hunt its prey; it simply had to be a little more streamlined than that. Also, it is rumoured that the experts consulted for the show gave the producers a weight of 50 tonnes for an 80-foot animal. The producers considered this a little unsensational and decided to size things up for themselves.

At this stage things were looking good for the fish and bad for the marine reptile. *Liopleurodon* was going to possess only a little more than half the length of its adversary and a fraction of the weight. It would surely seem sensible to replace *Liopleurodon* in this battle with one of the new and unknown pliosaurs based on the evidence from the lower jaws and vertebrae fragments. Then in December 2002 revelations concerning a startling discovery from Mexico came to light - enter the Monster of Aramberri.

Most media reported on this discovery with typical sensationalism – "a complete skeleton of the largest predator of all time, a Jurassic sea monster that made *Tyrannosaurus rex* look like a featherweight, has been discovered in Mexico" – said the *Times*.

These reports stated that the complete skeleton measured 64 feet from nose to tail and had been identified as a *Liopleurodon*. It boasted teeth the size of machetes packed into its ten-foot jaws and would have been capable of killing a blue whale. The skull, as large as a car, had huge holes in it, possibly inflicted by a victim that fought back.

The bones were discovered mingled with those of small ichthyosaurs (a prehistoric reptilian analogue of dolphins), which presumably formed past meals. "No other living creature in the sea could fight it successfully, it swallowed prey whole" said the leader of the research team.

The *Times* article went on to say that estimates prepared by the BBC for *Walking with Dinosaurs* suggest that the largest of the creatures would have been even bigger than the Monster of Aramberri, although it did add that most palaeontologists are more conservative than the BBC. It also added that the precise identification of *Liopleurodon* was not yet confirmed.

The numerous reports on the monster put out by the media make a very interesting study in 'Godzilla-isation' – the process whereby media accounts of the specimen inflate the size and ferocity until it has acquired an awesome list of characteristics. One particular noteworthy report stated that the creature could chew through granite!

In fact the very first estimate of size put the creature at around 50 feet in total length. This was based on a pectoral vertebrae and other bones being larger than that of *Kronosaurus*. This will clearly be revised as the specimen is prepared further and more knowledge comes to light. It also seems unlikely that the Monster of Aramberri is a *Liopleurodon*. *Liopleurodon* fossils to date have all been found in a concentrated area of northern Europe. That suggests it prowled those waters during its reign. The Monster of Aramberri was discovered a long way from *Liopleurodon's* other haunts. This alone might suggest that we are dealing with a completely different pliosaur. Furthermore, the age of the rock from which the Monster of Aramberri was plucked also suggests it was not a *Liopleurodon*. It puts it into the age of some other big pliosaurs known as *Pliosaurus, Stretosaurus* and *Megalneusaurus*.

The reconstruction of the Monster of Aramberri will apparently only begin after the animal has been completely excavated and in 2003 only about a sixth of the animal had emerged from the rock. It is an extremely labour-intensive business and the whole thing will take years. Interestingly, it was first discovered in 1982 by a Mexican student but was falsely interpreted as being the remains of a terrestrial dinosaur. A professor of palaeontology at Karlsruhe museum in Germany correctly assigned it to be a giant pliosaur. We now await more information from Karlsruhe.

In essence, there appears to be little evidence that *Liopleurodon* ever exceeded 35-40 feet in length. The 'move over *T. rex*' jibes often cited in popularist media should be dropped. *T. rex* can move back over now. Although reports of *Liopleurodon's* size may have been exaggerated, there always was tentative evidence of truly gigantic pliosaurs and the Monster of Aramberri seems to have upped the stakes somewhat. *Megalodon* may be swimming up and down her pool with impatience; but who exactly is she going to face off against?

Liopleurodon is clearly not our number one contender is this area. There is no evidence for *Liopleurodon* or any other pliosaur reaching 80 feet in length; *Kronosaurus, Pliosaurus, Stretosaurus* and *Megalneusarus* are all known from partial skeletons and heavy extrapolation of the available data. They were all in a similar size range to *Liopleurodon*. However, two specimens point to bigger pliosaurs. Firstly, a large lower jaw from the Oxford clays and secondly the Monster of Aramberri. Both of these creatures are currently unassigned. In the future, they may be described as a new pliosaur or they could be identified as larger specimens of an already identified pliosaur. Both specimens also suggest a creature in the region of 50 feet in total length.

Additionally, it must be noted that the Monster of Aramberri appears to have met its grisly end at the hands of another pliosaur. It has a four-inch bite mark in its skull, a strong indication of a fight to the death, where the Aramberri specimen came second. This could have been competition for a mate between the same species, or tantalisingly, it raises the possibility that the Monster of Aramberri was being predated on by an even larger marine reptile.

Given that the Aramberri creature is unlikely to have been the largest specimen of its kind and given that its conqueror may have been from an even larger species, suddenly the *Walking with Dinosaurs* figures do not seem too outlandish.

We know that large pliosaurs fed readily on ichthyosaurs and other long necked plesiosaurs. Their bones are often found together and many of their fossils bear the dentition marks of large pliosaurs. Research on *Liopleurodon* skulls suggests that it would have located its prey using its 'stereo nostrils'. These worked to detect the direction of movement and smells in the open water. As it swam with its mouth open, water would flow upward through scoop shaped holes in the roof of the mouth and out through the nostrils.

Pliosaurs had thick, conical teeth and were almost uniquely adapted for powerful biting. Estimates of biting force in excess of those produced by any living animal have been made for *T. rex*. This is based on the marks left on the bones of its prey/scavenged carcasses. The largest pliosaurs would appear to have been considerably larger and heavier than *T. rex* and therefore better adapted for powerful biting. A large pliosaur would have been able to hold a small car in its jaws and given that the back of its jaws were extended to make room for its large and powerful muscles, those teeth probably could have bitten through the lightweight steel of a modern car.

Given the plethora of different large pliosaurs and given that we can't be sure which one is which or whether the largest in our brood even has a name, we will simply refer to it as 'megapli'. It is hard to imagine that megapli had anything to fear from any other creature except perhaps its own kind. It certainly would have ruled the roost in its own time, but could the same be said throughout time?

MEGAPLI IN PROFILE

Length	Up to 70 feet
Weight	A cage fat 50 tonnes
Weaponry	Large stout conical teeth housed in a mouth ten feet long
Speed	Up to 15mph
Weaknesses	Mobility
Profile	Ichthyosaur and plesiosaur killer.
Human Champ	Poor Evander is used as a tooth pick. 'Nuff said!

BIG FIGHT BUILD UP

This one is so close to call, nobody dare call it. This fight prediction has been like a see-saw going one way then the other. Even the bookies are flummoxed.

The giant shark was looking a sure favourite when she was over a 100 feet in length and then someone went and pointed out all the problems with fitting all those teeth into one set of jaws and it was like an evil fairy had waved a magic wand – megalodon had shrunk by half. Still, at over 50 feet in length and possibly as long as 70 feet – megalodon was still an odds on favourite.

Then, just when we though megalodon was the true undisputed Daddy of the oceans, along came *Walking with Dinosaurs*. *Liopleurodon* was eating everything in its path. Ichthyosaurs were getting bitten in half, long-necked plesiosaurs were running for cover, sharks were swimming for their lives and even terrestrial dinosaurs weren't safe as giant *Liopleurodons* plucked them from the surf!

At over 80 feet in length and over 100 tonnes in weight, these *Liopleurodons* could use their ten-inch gnashers to crunch through granite (although why they should want to do this remains a mystery) and just about anything else that got in their way. Never mind Evander Holyfield, even Superman from the planet Krypton wouldn't be a match for this beast.

Just as we thought megalodon had become a mega-meal, those clever chaps came along and pointed out all those flaws again. Except in the case of *Liopleurodon*, the flaws came in multiples. There was in fact no proof that *Liopleurodon* ever achieved the sizes claimed by *Walking with Dinosaurs*. In fact, like megalodon, it halved in length overnight. Indeed, *Liopleurodon* wasn't even the size champion for its own kind. That particular title belonged to an antipodean cousin called *Kronosaurus* which was undergoing a downsizing of its own, reducing from just over 40 feet in length to more like 30 feet in length.

Things were looking bad for the pliosaurs as the pendulum swung again. All of a sudden they were looking like fish food. But dead they were not. Then came the news of the huge bits of bone in the Oxford clays suggesting pliosaurs of gigantic proportions. The pendulum swung back towards the *Walking with Dinosaurs* crew. However, pliosaur hopes were dashed again when one of the hopeful bones was identified as actually belonging to a sauropod dinosaur and actually had nothing to do with a pliosaur. Even if the remaining bone fragments were indeed from pliosaurs, the leading expert in the field was adamant that they did not come from a *Liopleurodon*. It was definitely being prepared as fish flakes and the identity of his larger cousins was definitely circumspect.

Megalodon was looking like the heavy betting favourite. The pliosaur camp was in disarray. They couldn't even decide who was going to represent them in the contest that could define their species. *Kronosaurus* and *Liopleurodon* bickered over each others credentials, whilst fiction writers gathered on the sidelines and pumped hot air into the belly of the *Liopleurodon* inflating its tonnage. All was well until its belly burst spilling forth sauropod bones that cracked the pliosaur management team over the head. Team pliosaur looked doomed whilst the large shark readied itself for a feast.

It was all over bar the shouting when the pendulum was resurrected and swung again. A discovery in Mexico of an as yet unnamed pliosaur suggested that the fiction writers might have been right after all! The Monster of Aramberri was born. The remains of a huge pliosaur began emerging from the rock. Early estimates gave the creature an overall body length approaching 60 feet. Suddenly megalodon again had a reason to be frightened.

Finally we have some stability. The two camps are ready. The combatants are of similar size and weight. Their weaponry, although different in design, are both immense and frightening. It's the conical shaped teeth with devastating crushing-power from megapli versus the super slashers from the jaws of megalodon. This really is an even affair and only a fool would bet big on this one. Let the titanic struggle commence....

SECONDS OUT

As both beasts approach one another the tension is evident. All other life-forms have scattered from the immediate vicinity including a twenty-five-foot shark that makes a modern great white look like a pussy cat. This is the ultimate clash of marine predators, crossing all boundaries of size and time. Both predators circle one another incredibly slowly. Speed is not the forte of either giant, but the respect and quite possibly fear of each other is strongly evident.

The circling continues unabated when suddenly, megapli sees a chink in the armour. It begins to flap its four huge paddles, attempting to fly through the water. The huge jaws gape as it makes a lunge for the rear end of the killer shark. Megalodon, sensing the danger, begins to accelerate as those killer jaws clamp shut on nothing but air and water. Megalodon has escaped the first assault.

The circling resumes in earnest, it is unclear whether that attempt at an assault has tired the big Pliosaur. Megalodon begins to slowly sink in depth. In response the pliosaur adjusts his position so he can keep an eye on his female adversary, but he doesn't attempt to follow. Megalodon continues to sink slowly, seemingly in retreat.

Suddenly, with a deafening silence megalodon flicks her huge tail, turns headlong and accelerates towards megapli like a streamlined torpedo. Caught unawares, megapli reacts a little late and tries to flap his way out of the oncoming missile. Yet the pliosaur's diversionary tactics are a little late. The shark makes contact and locks onto the underneath of the cage-fat body of his adversary, close to the rear left flipper.

Megapli opens those huge jaws in response, but is unable to extend his short neck around far enough to launch a counter offensive on his cartilaginous adversary. Megalodon, meanwhile, shakes her huge head from side to side gauging in the flesh. Finally a huge chunk of the reptilian hide is torn away, but the super shark loses a few of those six-inch teeth in the process, one of which remains embedded in the side of megapli.

Megalodon retreats quickly away from megapli and again begins to circle. Megapli remains motionless for a moment, almost paralysed by the ferocity of the attack, before managing to move slowly away in a lame attempt to flee. However, the shark's work is far from done and it begins to follow slowly. Megapli is bleeding profusely and acutely aware of the shark's presence. With another burst of speed megalodon again launches herself towards the pliosaur, this time however from the right side.

Megapli, though, is able to respond this time. Arcing his bleeding body, he opens those immense jaws as if to threaten the shark. Megalodon is in no hurry and aborts the attack, still wary despite megapli's injuries. However, the arcing defensive manoeuvres seem to have weakened megapli even further as he again seems paralysed in the water. Megalodon senses this momentary weakness and again launches another attack. Megapli is slow to respond and megalodon again locks her teeth onto the body of the pliosaur eventually removing another chunk from the flesh.

Megalodon again hastily retreats and begins circling the pliosaur. Megapli now has two gaping wounds and slowly begins to sink, making only spasmodic musculatory movements. Megalodon closes in again, still keeping away from those huge jaws as she severs the vast majority of the rear right flipper. A further three attacks occur before megapli breathes his last.

Megalodon has defeated megapli, but her dominance is far from supreme. In the event of a rematch, the result would be just as uncertain. If megapli had secured the first strike, the result would likely have been reversed. Both remain Daddies of the oceans (or Mummy in megalodon's case) and in the light of current knowledge, neither emerges as a clear favourite over the other.

Chapter 5 – Deep in the Ocean
Sperm Whale vs. Giant Squid

MOBY DICK

Thus far we have dealt with the greatest predators in the oceans through two different eras. Nobody would argue that orcas, great white sharks, megalodon and pliosaurs are, and were, all apex predators in their own right. But were they the ultimate animal Daddy? What constitutes a predator? What makes a great hunter? Invariably, things come down to size and weight. The bigger a creature, the easier it often is to overwhelm the prey items. Blue whales are probably the largest creatures that have ever lived, yet they are not really active hunters by our definition of the word. They may eat living zooplankton and krill, but their method of harvesting their prey is more akin to filtration than hunting. The afore-mentioned hunters represent the power and aggression shown by an active predator. Megalodon and the pliosaurs may well represent the largest predators of all time. However, they may both be eclipsed by a creature alive, well and swimming in today's oceans. Orcas do not have a monopoly in the large, potentially aggressive toothed whale department. The sperm whale may in fact be the largest and heaviest predator to have ever lived!

Hermann Melville's classic tale *Moby Dick* tells of the almost mythical pursuit of a white sperm whale. Written well before *Jaws* or even its author was conceived, Moby Dick fights back against his pursuers and manages to bring about the sinking of a large whaling vessel. Although the account is fictional, the accounts from *Moby Dick* were not written loosely without any basis. Many a whaler told of the almighty aggression displayed by sperm whales whenever they were harpooned.

Still, generally speaking, we don't think of the sperm whale as an active and aggressive predator. It doesn't approach our beaches and eat surfers or bathers, it doesn't capsize ships; in fact we think of it more as an intelligent, fluffy almost cuddly creature that we could take home and put in a large garden pond. Is there really an argument for it being the greatest predator that ever lived?

Well, yes in fact, there is. The sperm whale is by far the largest of the odontocetes, or toothed whales. Its scientific name, *Physeter macrocephalus*, literally means 'big-headed blower'. It acquired its name 'sperm' whale from the milky liquid wax in its head, whalers likening it to the fluid produced by the testes to carry sperm. Although the name is used throughout the English-speaking world, many other nations refer to this giant as 'cachalot'. This derives from the Catalan word meaning big teeth. There is a large difference in body size between the sexes in sperm whales. Females average about 35 feet in total body length, rarely ever exceeding forty feet. Males on the other hand average about fifty feet in total length and the largest recorded length for an adult bull sperm whale was just shy of 68 feet. It is estimated that the average adult male weighs in at around 45 tonnes with females being less than half that. The largest animal reliably weighed was a 60-foot male that weighed a huge 57 tonnes.

Sperm whales are usually dark brown or grey in colour, often looking completely black in poor light. Older males often have large numbers of scars on their heads, deriving from fights with other males or from the hooks and suckers of squid; their preferred prey in most areas.

The profile of the sperm whale is unlike any other species. It has a rectangular head, which is already a quarter of the body length at birth. The head grows disproportionately until it is a third of the total length in adult bulls. The lower jaw is roughly cylindrical for much of its length and in an adult holds 50 rounded conical teeth in two parallel rows. These range between three and eight inches in length. They are the largest teeth of any animal species recognised as being alive today and may weigh over a kilogramme each. Indeed, the largest known tooth from a sperm whale measures an impressive eleven inches. Sperm whales have two short, stubby flippers at the back of their heads, which means that their method of propulsion is not the most efficient. Maximum speed is around the six miles per hour mark. However, their triangular tail flukes are large and powerful. As well as a means of locomotion, their tails can just as easily be used as a dangerous weapon.

Sperm whales are essentially oceanic animals, normally venturing close to shore only when sick or the depth of water increases rapidly away from the coast (such as a volcanic island). Males can withstand a wide range of temperatures from the warmth of the tropics to the chill of the polar regions. Females and young, however, remain in warmer waters. The basic social unit is considered to be a family group of ten to twenty animals, primarily adult females with their offspring of various ages. Males usually leave the group at puberty and become less social as they get older. They sometimes join a 'bachelor' pod of medium sized males before becoming a 'lone' bull wandering the world's oceans.

In most areas where they occur, sperm whales feed almost exclusively on cephalopods (that is squid and octopus). Prey is taken at considerable depths, frequently in excess of 1000 feet and generally in midwater. However, bottom feeding is indicated by the capture of fish and octopi living exclusively on or near the seabed. Contrary to popular belief, most of the squid taken is not the giant squid of legend and the whale's adversary here. Instead medium sized squid between one and ten feet in total length form the bulk of the diet. Fish species eaten include rays, sharks, lanternfish and members of the cod family. It is estimated that sperm whales consume about three per cent of their body weight a day, nearly 1.5 tonnes in an adult male. That's a lot of squid! Larger sperm whales obviously take larger prey, feed at greater depths and dive for longer periods. Indeed, the depth record in the animal kingdom is held by a sperm whale. A 47-foot bull was recorded at 1134 metres, discovered with its jaw entangled in a submarine cable. Yet this is only the *recorded* depth record. In 1969 a bull was killed 100 miles south of Durban in South Africa after it had surfaced from a dive lasting an hour and 52 minutes. In its stomach were two small sharks eaten about an hour earlier. The sharks were later identified as a species that only lives on the sea floor. At that distance from land the depth of the water exceeds 1,000 feet for a radius of 30-40 miles. When seeking food the sperm whale would appear to be more limited by pressure of time rather than pressure of pressure!

The largest accurately measured specimen on record was a bull measuring 67 feet, 11 inches (20.7m), captured off the Kurile Islands in the northwest Pacific. This individual was caught by a USSR whaling fleet in 1950. However, much larger individuals were reported from the early days of whaling and these may have spawned the *Moby Dick* legend. Indeed, it seems reasonable to assume that many of the largest whales would have succumbed to the whaling industry leaving us with a somewhat smaller population, relatively undersized compared to the recent past. In the British museum of natural history in London a lower jaw of a sperm whale is exhibited exceeding sixteen feet in length. It is alleged that the jaw came from an 84-foot specimen and similar lengths have been reported for other outsized individuals that were killed. If such lengths are accurate, it probably exceeds those of even the largest megalodon and pliosaurs. Also, the weight of such a large specimen could be estimated in the region of 90-100 tonnes, quite possibly making it the heaviest active predator to have ever roamed the earth.

If one does an internet search various cryptozoological groups with message boards debate some of the issues discussed throughout this book. I remember one such 'debate' between internet protagonists. One was making the case for megalodon as the greatest oceanic predator; the other was making the case for the sperm whale. The megalodoner argued the case for his man based on its devastating bite, its mobility, manoeuvrability and of course its immense size. The whaler retorted by acknowledging some of the points raised but countered on issues of size and weight alone. Megalodon in his opinion was a mere fifty-foot fish, whereas the sperm whale grew to twice that length. Both virtual cornermen quoted various pages from an online encyclopaedia to each other on the statistics and capabilities of their champion elect. However, their 'facts' related mainly to hearsay and possibles not cold, testable claims. The claim of sperm whales reaching over 100 feet in total length was not backed up with hard fact, but instead with claims of whalers from the 18th and 19th centuries.

Unlike our prehistoric quarry, there is less room for speculation here. We have harvested sperm whales for their blubber and oil. Tourists watch them from boats, we make wildlife documentaries on them, tag them, follow them on sonar and their carcasses wash up on beaches. We have a reasonable idea of their anatomy and size based on numerous specimens and observations. Certainly, the individuals today are smaller than yesteryear. The butchery of the whaling industry decimated populations and killed many of the finest specimens. The largest ever sperm whale is probably not alive today and was probably caught during the height of the whaling years. However, 80-foot specimens almost certainly did exist. The mandibles from the British Museum specimen add further weight to these claims. But 100 footers appear, at least to this writer, to be stretching things somewhat and take it more into the realm of fishermen's tales of 'the one that got away'. Eyewitness testimony is such a shaky foundation on which to base size claims. For example, I remember boarding a tourist boat on Loch Ness and the captain proceeded to inform me that he regularly saw a 15-foot pike in the loch. That is a fish with an upper size range in the region of six feet, yet he was claiming Loch Ness had one the size of a great white shark. Amazingly, he seemed offended by my incredulity!

Nonetheless, with all the evidence available to us, the sperm whale probably represents the largest single predator ever to have roamed planet earth. Still, this dilemma remains. Orcas and white sharks do not live in fear of the sperm whale. Most other large denizens of the deep do not fear them. Divers frequently swim with them. Yet they can show remarkable aggression to each other and when attacked. Whalers and fishermen have told tales of clashes between two large bull sperm whales that often end with the loser quite badly wounded. The sperm whale represents a gentle giant with a dark side. It has nothing to fear from any singular predator in the ocean, but is it invincible? Perhaps not. Enter the legendary Kraken….

SPERM WHALE IN PROFILE

Length	Up to 85 feet
Weight	Up to 100 tonnes
Weaponry	Over 50 strong, stout conical teeth, reaching 11 inches in length
Speed	6 mph
Weaknesses	Very slow
Profile	A gentle giant (mostly). However, if you're a squid be afraid, be very afraid....
Human Champ	Evander Holyfield lets leash with his best 5 punch combination. The whale presumably takes this to be a token of affection and returns the compliment with a flick of its huge tale flukes, which smash 3 of Holyfield's ribs (by accident). Holyfield begins to drown and is plucked from the water, thankful that the whale didn't decide to give him kiss!

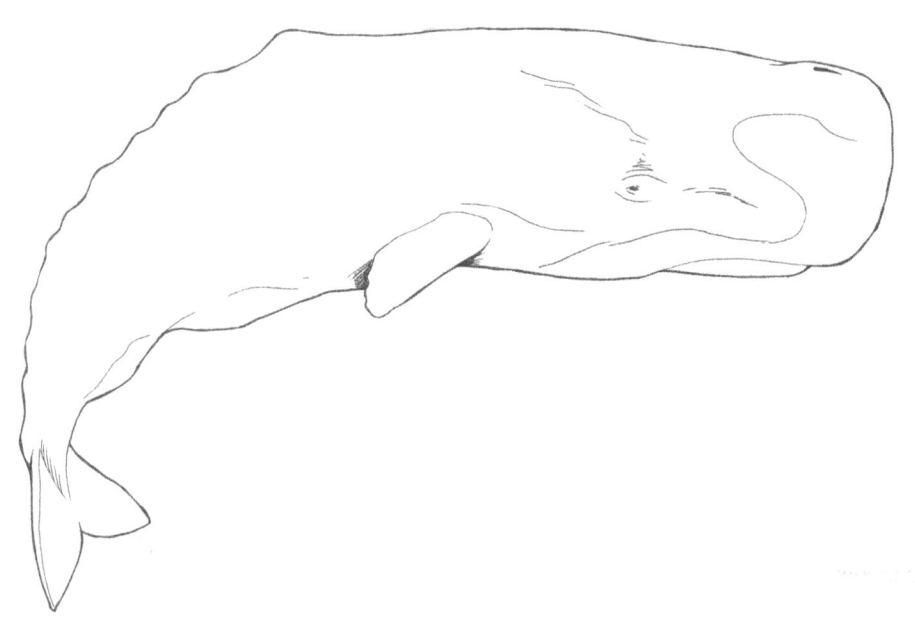

THE KRAKEN

It has often been said in the popular literature that the sperm whales feeds on the giant squid (*Architeuthis dux*); that the squid is the favourite food of the whale, etc. However, the only proof of this is the stomach contents of certain whales, which have contained remains of some giant squid. Nobody (apart from a few mariners' claims - to be discussed later) has ever witnessed this epic clash of marine giants.

In fact we know virtually nothing about the history of the giant squid. It occasionally washes ashore and when that happens we don't know why. Its feeding habits, breeding habits, vertical and geographic distribution, life span and habitat are all unknown. For all we know about it, the giant squid might as well live on the moon!

The giant squid is one of the largest animals in the world, yet we have no idea how big it actually gets. The size of the giant squid has long been a topic for speculation amongst scientists, seamen, whalers and authors. To refer back to our bible for size maximums, the *Guinness Book of Records* tells us that the Thimble Tickle specimen of 1879 measured 55 feet from mantle to tentacle tip. However, more recently it has been suggested that the original source material contained a typographic error and that the animal was no more than 35 feet in length.

However, I remember watching the serious *Mysterious World* featuring the Sci-Fi writer Arthur C. Clarke during the late 80s. He pointed out quite correctly that it is highly unlikely that the world's biggest squid had been among the very few cast ashore to be examined and measured by naturalists. Indeed, the programme also contained an interview with the now deceased Frederick Aldrich, a teuthologist (squid expert). Aldrich was shown examining an immature 20 foot giant squid specimen and he then postulated that the giant squid could reach an approximate maximum length of 150 feet! Now in previous chapters we have emphasised how science is often the search for funding rather than the search for facts. Aldrich may have been exaggerating his personal beliefs for the cameras, but given that we know so little about these giants there is also some basis for his claims.

The giant squid is such a spectacular animal, that those that include it in their catalogue of monsters often find it easy to increase its size substantially. In a book on dangerous sea creatures, for example, Thomas Dozier introduces his discussion by saying that two 42-foot tentacles were vomited up by a captive whale in an aquarium. Experts calculated that it had to have belonged to a monster weighing over 38 tonnes (!) and over 66 feet in length. Also, he discusses sperm whales with tentacle marks eighteen inches across, which he postulates would have had to have been inflicted by a gargantuan squid of at least 200 feet. The father of cryptozoology, Bernard Heuvelmans, in a more scientific tome, suggested that there were good reasons to believe that specimens existed twice as long as the Thimble Tickle squid and depending on girth would probably have weighed around 64 tonnes!

Although the length estimates given above can be debated, the weight estimates are far too generous. Firstly, the total length of the giant squid from mantle to tentacle tip, although not inflated, gives a false impression. The main body of the squid represents about a quarter of this total length. Its eight arms then represent about another quarter length. The two thin tentacles then represent the remaining half of the total body length. Thus, even if the squid possessed the bodily structure of a large mammal, a 60-footer, in weight terms, represents only about half that. Secondly, the flesh of giant squid is saturated with ammonium chloride, which means that it is actually lighter than water (hence dead or dying squid are found floating or washed up). The bodies of giant squid will be therefore be considerably lighter than normal mammalian skeletons.

Some zoologists, crypto or otherwise, believe only in those creatures (or their dimensions) that can be empirically confirmed and verified. Bernard Heuvelmans is from a different school of thought completely. He would argue that anything can exist at almost any size, because nobody can prove otherwise. His position on large giant squid is that all the reports of huge arm fragments, sightings at sea and even attacked ships cannot all be hoaxes, misidentifications or typographical errors. His position in the case of the giant squid is virtually untenable as so little is known about the creature. So what have we got in terms of alleged reports on the creature?

In 1946 a story appeared in the respectable Norwegian journal *Naturen* (translated as Nature) concerning how a 15,000 tonne freighter was attacked by a giant squid. As the ship was 500ft long it had little to fear and the squid, unable to get a grip on the hull, skidded along until it ended up in the propeller where it was ground to pieces. Accounts of giant squid attacking ships are not unique but they are rare.

An account from 1874 states that the schooner, *Pearl,* was attacked and sunk by a giant squid whilst sailing in the Bay of Bengal. Witnesses spoke of how a great mass rose out of the sea and attacked the ship. If the account is to be believed, it cannot have been a small creature that carried out the attack.

There are a few accounts of 100-foot+ squid in the literature either washed up or seen alive by witnesses. In a 1973 paper, scientists Paul Leblond and John Siebert relate a story told to them by a Charles Dudoward. It concerns the washing up of a huge squid in 1922 in front of a hotel. They were supplied with a drawing, which seemingly showed a large cephalopod on the lawn of the hotel. It was described as "having four arms on either side fifty feet long… but the one in the middle was about 100 feet long and may have been longer when stretched". Leblond and Siebert noted the similarities between the descriptions of giant squid found on Newfoundland's beaches at the end of the nineteenth century and concluded the creature must have been a giant squid.

There are numerous further accounts in Michael Bright's book *There are Giants in the Sea* concerning very large squid. In 1926 a badly damaged carcass, which locals claimed to be a giant squid was washed ashore on the Natal coast of South Africa. Although the arms and tentacles were missing, the estimates based on the size of the body alone put the overall length at around 100 feet. Others found washed up in Newfoundland were supposedly measured at 72 feet and 88 feet respectively. However, these are unverified claims and cannot be taken as fact. Bright also refers to an account that if true, is amazing. It concerns a squid that supposedly appeared alongside a trawler lying off the Maldive Islands in the Indian Ocean. The witness was J.D. Starkey who often fished at night over the stern of the ship using a cluster of light bulbs. One night as he walked the deck he had an unusual visitor:

> 'The water appeared to become opaque as something filled my view. As I gazed fascinated, a circle of green light glowed in my area of illumination. The green unwinking orb, I suddenly realised was an eye [the giant squid has eyes the size of large dinner plates]. The surface of the water undulated with some strange disturbance. Gradually, I realized that I was gazing at almost point-blank range at a huge squid. I say huge, the word should be colossal, as so far all I could see was the body and that alone filled my view as far as the eye could penetrate...... I took my quartermaster's torch and shining it into the water I walked forward. I climbed the ladder and shone the torch downwards. There in a pool of light were its tentacles. I would not exaggerate a natural phenomenon, but these were at least 24 inches thick. The suction discs could clearly be seen. ......I walked aft keeping the squid in view. This was not difficult as it was lying alongside the ship, quite still except for a pulsing movement. As I approached the stern where my bulb cluster was hanging there was the body. Every detail was visible, the valve through which the creature appeared to breathe and the parrot like beak. Gradually the truth dawned, I had walked the entire length of the ship, 175 feet plus.....after 15 minutes it seemed to swell as its valve opened fully and without any visible effort it zoomed, if I may use the expression into the night'.

Starkey sent his account to a magazine called *Animals* in response to an article the magazine had run on sea serpents. The magazine summed it all up quite well when they wrote:

> 'The giant squids are among the most remarkable, and at the same time, among the least known creatures that live in the sea. From what little we know of them they appear to inhabit the middle depths of the oceans [not the abysmal depths], but many deep sea creatures move towards the surface at night, and Mr. Starkey's observation suggests that these great molluscs may be among them.....A squid of the enormous size recorded by Mr Starkey is not beyond the bounds of possibility and we welcome the privilege of putting this remarkable adventure on record'.

Starkey's story is remarkable and notably understated in its description. I certainly found myself wanting to believe his observations and not being drawn to believe we had a hoax or gross exaggeration. However, the length of the creature described is remarkable (175 feet plus) and is still a little difficult to swallow.

A similar account was received by Richard Ellis, the author of the *Search for the Giant Squid*. Ellis is not drawn to hyperbole and is a very thorough researcher with a conservative outlook on most claims. After he had appeared on a television programme claiming that nobody had ever seen a live giant squid he received a letter from a Dennis Braun. Braun stated that as a nineteen-year-old Marine Corporal he was on an amphibious assault training exercise near Puerto Rico. Again, sailors were fishing off the side of the ship when he became aware of an enormous squid that had come to rest on the sandy bottom beside the ship.

Very matter-of-fact, he stated that he could only guess at the dimensions but stated that it was *much* larger than the squid from the TV Programme (30 feet). He stated that the water must have been at least fifty feet deep to house the ship and that he was about thirty feet above the water from his vantage point. The water had perfect clarity and he estimated that in order to scan the entire body length he had to rotate his eyes thirty degrees in both directions. Given the information provided he stated that it was probably at least 100 feet in length.

Richard Ellis spoke to Dennis Braun and he was totally innocent of the controversy that surrounds the giant squid. In fact, although the squid was very large he had no reason to assume that it was in any way unusual. Indeed, this account moved Ellis so much that he revised some of his previous estimates and began to concede the possibility that 100-foot giants existed after all (he still maintained that 150-200-footers were outlandish and would have too much of a difficult time finding food).

In 2004 a giant squid was caught on film for the first time in its natural habitat. Using a robotic camera at a depth of 3000 feet, two Japanese scientists managed to lure a twenty-six-foot specimen using bait. The researchers concluded that *Architeutis* seems to be a much more active predator than previously expected, using its elongate feeding tentacles to strike and tangle prey. They reported that the tentacles would apparently coil into a ball, much as a python would envelop its victims.

The researchers created a float system with a long line from which they suspended a robotic camera and strobe light. The camera looked downwards at hooks baited with small squid and took pictures every thirty seconds. A bag of mashed shrimps acted as an odour lure. On Sept. 30th 2004, a squid attacked the lowest bait on a rig that was positioned about 1,000 feet above the sea floor. During the attack the squid wrapped its two long tentacles around the bait.

One of the squid's tentacles was caught, and the creature moved violently in the next four hours to break free. It was often out of camera range, suggesting, the scientists say, that it was attempting to swim free. After four hours, thirteen minutes of struggle, the animal tore away, leaving a tentacle behind. At 26 feet, this may be a relatively small specimen; but DNA analysis confirmed it as *Architeuthis*.

Captured sperm whales are often scarred by what appears to have been suckers on the arms of large squid. Since it is known that sperm whales have a preference for squid of all sizes it seems reasonable to assume that the scars were caused by squid that didn't like the idea of being eaten.

In a 1912 book entitled *Depths of the Ocean*, Johann Hjort made one of the most quoted and equally misquoted remarks ever made about the giant squid. Inspecting a dead sperm whale, he noted a number of circular scars, which it occurred to him, must be the marks left by the suckers of large squid. He measured the largest of these marks to be just over an inch in diameter, but also found in the whale's mouth a piece of squid tentacle seven inches in diameter. A photograph of these marks appears in the book with the caption 'skin of a cachalot with marks from the struggle with *Architeuthis*'. The picture has been reproduced in many a discussion of sperm whales and squid, yet the size of the circular scars has continued to grow. This is possibly because of confusion over the one-inch marks and the seven inch tentacle.

In the *Time Life* book *Dangerous Sea Creatures* it states that an ordinary giant squid leaves teeth ringed sucker marks up to four inches across, whilst the *Guinness Book of Animal Facts and Feats* describes scarring up to five inches in diameter. An article in *Exotic Zoology* even made claims for a mark two feet in diameter!

Marine biologist and teuthologist Malcolm Clarke wrote that although the largest circular scars on sperm whales came from *Architeuthis*, the squid with the largest suckers, he had yet to see conclusive evidence to suggest that any of the sucker scars were larger than 1.5 inches. Yet to counteract this, a 1938 monograph by L Harrison Matthews on sperm whales stated that scars caused by suckers were regularly up to four inches. However, this is much larger than other recorded sucker dimensions.

So in the light of all this data, what can we conclude? Will *Architeuthis* live up to the kraken legend?

Well, maybe it doesn't have to. In 2003, it was widely reported in the popular press that the giant squid, *Architeuthis dux* was no longer the largest squid that was known to science. The first example of *Mesonychoteuthis hamiltoni* had just been retrieved virtually intact from the ocean surface in Antarctic waters.

Although it was known to science from 1925, all of the previous five specimens were known only from bit parts recovered from the stomachs of sperm whales. This relative newcomer is being commonly referred to as the 'colossal squid.'

The scientist responsible was analysing the new specimen was adamant that 'the giant squid is no longer the largest squid out there. We've got something even larger and not just larger, but, an order of magnitude meaner". The colossal squid had a particularly large beak and unique swivelling hooks on the clubs at the ends of its tentacles. It was claimed that this combination would allow it to attack fish as large as the Patagonian toothfish (about six feet in length) and probably to also 'attempt to maul' sperm whales.

Dr O'Shea claimed that the new specimen had a larger mantle length than any giant squid specimen he had ever seen and furthermore, that the new specimen was still a juvenile (based on an analysis of and lack of prior sexual activity), at probably only half its adult size. For his part Richard Ellis chipped in and stated that he considered the colossal squid no more a monster than the giant squid.

So has the giant squid been removed from his lofty squid perch or is this another case of a scientist exaggerating claims to obtain a larger funding grant?

Anecdotally, the colossal squid would seem to have a case. The two species are quite distinct in their shape and profile. If the mantle length were the same in a giant squid and a colossal squid, then the giant squid would be the larger creature, possessing longer tentacles and arms. Yet the maximum mantle length for the colossal squid would seem to exceed that of the giant squid, thus giving it a greater overall length. Also, the colossal squid is proportionately bulkier, probably giving it a greater weight when compared to the giant squid.

Also, it has often been claimed that the verified and measured size record for the giant squid (55 feet) may have been exaggerated because of a lengthening (stretching like rubber bands) of the very slight tentacular arms. The recently captured specimen of the colossal squid had a greater mantle length.

In February 2007 the colossal squid seemed to verify its claims to be the new squid-size king. It was announced by authorities in New Zealand that the largest known colossal squid had been captured. The specimen weighed 495kg and was initially estimated to measure 10m (33 feet) in total length.

Fishermen caught the animal in freezing Antarctic waters. It was brought to the surface as it fed on an Antarctic toothfish that had been caught off a long line. It would not let go of its prey and could not be removed from the line by the fishermen so they decided to catch it instead. They managed to envelop it in a net, hauled it aboard and froze it. The specimen eclipsed the previous largest find in 2003 by about 195kg. However, it is still considerably smaller than some estimates have predicted and its beak was a lot smaller than other squid beaks that have been recovered from the stomachs of sperm whales.

Yet what of these alleged sightings of enormous squid over and above 100 feet in length? If we even believe these claims at all, were they representatives of the giant, colossal or even an as yet unidentified squid? As the witnesses were not knowledgeable in this small, relatively unknown scientific field, we will probably never know. It seems unlikely that they were colossal squid. Despite the claims made earlier in this chapter, most recent size estimates for both species are far more cautious, suggesting a maximum length of 43 feet for the giant squid and 46 feet for the colossal squid.

As far as we can tell thus far, they belong in cold southern waters around Antarctica and New Zealand. However, we know so little about large squid that their range may be vast and span the entire globe. Even in the tropics the water is cold and dark in the depths so there seems no logical reason for the squid to be rooted to a particular area.

For the purposes of this contest, we will refer to our cephalopod king as the champion squid and send it forth to fight the sperm whale.

CHAMPION SQUID – IN PROFILE

Length	Claimed to be over 100 feet
Weight	Unknown. A 50ft specimen very unlikely to exceed a tonne
Weaponry	A large razor-sharp beak and numerous claw-like hooks emerging from tentacle suckers.
Speed	Probably exceeding 30mph in short bursts
Weaknesses	A lack of weight
Profile	The kraken of legend and a creature from which nightmares spawn. It could be an alien from another world and given what we know about it, it might as well be.
Human Champ	Evander Holyfield doesn't even have time to let leash a combination before he is enveloped by those long arms and his flesh and innards are torn to pieces by those long hooks on the end of the suckers. His soft remains are then pulled in and shredded by the sharp beak.

BIG FIGHT BUILD UP

The sperm whale starts a heavy betting favourite in this match up. Widely regarded as probably the largest, heaviest toothed predator of all time, with a terrible temper when troubled, the champion squid will have to be on top form to avoid being eaten. Furthermore, squid ranging in size from small to pretty large are known to make up a large proportion of the sperm whale's diet. Given this, is there any hope for the champion squid?

Bernard Heuvelmans refers to an incident in his book *The Wake of the Sea Serpents,* which may make a case for the squid. A mariner reported an incident where he claims he witnessed a large squid attacking a sperm whale. In his work of fiction *The Beast, Jaws* author Peter Benchley describes an outsized squid killing a juvenile sperm whale. Unfortunately for the squid, even in this work of fiction the monstrous tentacled behemoth finally meets its end in the jaws of a sperm whale. If I were you, I'd bet your house and your life savings on Moby Dick.

SECONDS OUT

Often in these situations the protagonists approach each other cautiously, first sizing each other up, assessing each other's strengths and weaknesses. The sperm whale simply isn't interested in protocol. He makes a beeline for the 100-foot squid. At 70 feet in length himself, he is an old bull used to this scenario. The squid might be longer than him, but he is heavier and stronger.

The squid sees the hulking dark shape emerge from the gloom and immediately retreats in an explosive burst. Stressed by this hulking mass, the squid is undergoing a colour change, attempting in vain to disguise itself and crucially, prevent itself from becoming calamari.

This process repeats itself several times. The whale approaches: slow; steady; unrelenting. The squid retreats in a burst of speed only for the whale to continue its relentless pursuit.

It becomes obvious to the squid that it will never outrun its tormentor. The whale will not be deterred. This time when it approaches, the squid attacks its nemesis, wrapping it tentacles around the head of the black hulk. Those massive suckers on the arms are definitely going to sting where it rips at the flesh. Unfortunately for the squid, the whale manages to get a grip on the mantle of the squid with those massive conical teeth. It begins to pull the squid further and further into its giant maw. Despite sustaining some battle wounds and some long-term scars to keep, calamari is on the menu after all….

Chapter 6
Living "Dinosaurs"
Komodo Dragon vs. Anaconda

DRAGON

So we move on to a completely new category: clash of the "living dinosaurs". By this we mean creatures whose ancestry is prehistoric and whose appearance conjures up images of beasts from a completely different era. For this we start with the Komodo dragon or to give them their local name, 'Ora.' The Komodo dragon, although not a dragon in the mythical sense (a huge fire-breathing creature with wings), is not a creature to be sneered at. It is actually the world's biggest recognised surviving lizard (you may well remember that the word dinosaur means 'terrible lizard'). It belongs to a family that includes 52 species of monitor lizards.

Komodo dragons live almost exclusively on four small south-eastern Indonesian Islands (Flores, Komodo, Rinca and Gili Montang) so unless you specifically set out with the express intention of finding one, you are unlikely ever to meet one (except possibly in a zoo). I once set out on a wild expedition to Indonesian to search for a legendary creature called orang pendek, the alleged apeman of the western Sumatran jungles. The trip turned out to be much wilder than I had hoped when our guide managed to get us lost in the uninhabitable, mountainous, and treacherous terrain. Four days without food ensued as we hacked down jungle, became entangled in thickets and crossed wild rivers in an attempt to find civilisation. My altimeter informed us that we dropping height and on the fourth day we encountered an illegal logger who directed our guide to his camp and his fellow illegal loggers. We became the centre of attention for these jungle people. They had never before seen a white person and they also didn't believe our guide when he told them where we had come from. They said no living person had ever trekked through the jungle from whence we came. They directed us through another 60km of jungle and we escaped from the jungle's clutches back to civilisation.

Whilst I was lost it was both the most frightening and yet exhilarating experience of my life. We were lost in the world's second largest expanse of rainforest. It was completely untouched by man and completely unexplored. Without food we would soon perish and our ability to catch live food was non-existent. We had probably a couple of weeks before we would die, therefore the urgency to escape was paramount. My brain was wired and prioritised to flee our current surroundings. We weren't stopping to take photographs. However, I remember the terrain and experience vividly. This was no walk in the forest and we took risks in crossing river rapids and descending waterfalls that in everyday life we would never have taken. The difference was we *had* to take those risks because they were preferable to remaining where we were.

Despite our predicament, whilst trudging through the jungle I couldn't help but marvel at our surroundings. It was just how I imagined a prehistoric forest to be and I was struck by how easy it would be for something large and unknown to science to live in those forests, undetected and unknown to man. Needless to say, we never did find any evidence of *orang pendek*. I spoke to a couple of witnesses, believers who had never seen it and non-believers alike. I spoke to jungle people who had never seen it, but they had never seen a Sumatran tiger either, such is their rarity and endangered status. Whilst we were lost we were fortunate enough to see fresh tiger tracks in the jungle interior, but no tiger (probably just as well).

Upon escaping from the Sumatran jungle we travelled to another part of Indonesia and spent a week on a beach in Bali. Whilst in Bali, we were offered the opportunity of a boat trip to the island of Komodo. Naturally my ears pricked up at the very mention of it. I knew what the island offered. However, we rejected the opportunity in the end. It involved a three-day sail and about another $1500 dollars, money we just didn't have to spare. Furthermore, after the Sumatran experience we had probably had enough adventure for that week. We settled instead, for a trip to a Balinese zoo where I got to see a baby Komodo (about three feet long) and feel the weight on my shoulders of a thirteen foot python. However, I couldn't stop wondering what prehistoric creatures would have been waiting to meet us on Komodo's beaches. As the world's heaviest lizard the Komodo dragon has a long body, well developed legs and deeply forked tongue that it flicks out when it searches for food. Juveniles are boldly marked with grey or cream bands, but they lose these markings as they mature. They soon become uniformly greyish brown in colour, with scaly, thickly folded skin.

Dragons live on scrubby hillsides, in open woodland and dry river beds where they feed on both living animals and carrion, wherever they can find it. They can detect the scent of decaying remains from up to three miles away. In addition to their scavenging they are also ambush predators. Young dragons will attack and eat snakes, other lizards and rodents. Adults target much larger prey. These include deer, wild boar, water buffalo and occasionally stray human tourists. They are also cannibalistic, which is one reason why young dragons spend much of their time in trees, where the heavier adults cannot reach them. Dragons have excellent eyesight, but they find most of their food by smell. Like snakes, they 'taste' the air with their tongues, collecting scent molecules from the air. They have sharp, serrated teeth, but cannot chew. Instead, they tear off pieces of food and then throw them backwards into their mouths. Although it has recently been discovered that they are mildly venomous, the saliva of the Komodo dragon is rich in toxic bacteria that thrive on traces of flesh, and the bacteria are far more dangerous than the venom. The bacteria are so virulent that the wounds of a victim will often simply not heal. As a result, when a dragon bites its prey these bacteria contaminate the wound. Even if a victim does not die from the initial attack it often dies from the resulting infection. Curiously, Komodo dragons seem to be immune to the effects of their own bacteria. Thus, although they are cannibalistic, smaller Komodos need not fear a bacterial injury.

Accordingly, Komodo dragons cannot really be referred to as a devastating power predator. It won't knock the head from the shoulders of its victim or bite it in half at the first attempt. Frequently, ambushed prey escapes from its clutches only to succumb several hours or even days later as the bacterial effect of the bite takes hold. Guided by scent, the dragon will find the last resting place of its victim and hone in on the signal, allowing it to feed. It has unusually flexible joints between its jaw and skull enabling it to swallow large chunks of food. Watching this behaviour reminds us of another prehistoric survivor – the crocodilians. The dragon will feed rapidly, swallowing flesh, skin and even bones. It will have limited time before other dragons converge on the carcass. As more dragons arrive at the scene of a kill, the larger animals will often try and intimidate the smaller ones into backing away. If food is scarce, fighting will often break out. Adult dragons are mainly solitary creatures although they often converge at the site of a kill. During the breeding season males compete for the chance to mate, wrestling with each other in an upright position, their tails acting as props. Females dig nests in the sand

and lay up to twenty-five eggs. Nine months later when the eggs hatch the baby dragons are left to fend for themselves. These living dinosaurs show no motherly love. Komodo dragons take about five years to become sexually mature and have a lifespan of about 40 years.

Male and female Komodo dragons are not strikingly different in appearance, the main distinguishing feature being size. Adult females weigh less and are shorter in length, typically reaching about seven to eight feet in length and 150 lbs in weight. Males, however, commonly exceed nine feet and outsized specimens have been claimed to reach eleven to twelve feet in length. An exceptionally large male could also potentially weigh as much as 600lbs after a large meal. The largest accurately measured specimen was a male presented to a U.S. zoologist by the Sultan of Bima in 1928. In 1937 it was ten feet, two inches long and 365lbs.

By weight, Komodos are the world's largest lizard, with their long thick tales sometimes half their body length. A hardy constitution has enabled them to survive for millions of years as the apex predator in an environment that has proved inhospitable to other meat-eaters. Komodos are also excellent swimmers, allowing them to travel between islands in search of food or mates. When attacking large prey, dragons typically inflict terrible bites on the feet and lower legs. It has been claimed that they take down prey as large as a 1300lb water buffalo. Smaller prey is usually snapped up with a quick lunge led with wide-open jaws. Like most reptiles, Komodos have a low resting metabolic rate and studies have shown that even a large individual could survive on as little as 1lb of meat per day. However, they can eat up to 80% of their body weight at a single meal, meaning they may not need to eat again for weeks on end. Komodos can be pretty explosive and for short distances can reach speeds of up to 15 mph. Also, they are a fairly recent discovery. Komodos were unknown to the western world until 1912. Early in the twentieth century westerners began to hear native stories of a 'land crocodile' said to inhabit some Indonesian islands. In 1912 a party of pearl fisherman reported that they had encountered a prehistoric beast on one of the islands on their travels. A team from a Javanese zoological museum was duly dispatched and they published the first report on the creature. In 1926 a team from the American natural history museum captured two live specimens and returned to America with a dozen dead ones. Indeed, it has been said that the arrival of Komodos in New York in the 1920s inspired the Hollywood production of King Kong!

The Komodo dragon may be the largest lizard alive today, but it did have a much larger antipodean cousin from the fairly recent prehistoric past. The remains of *Megalania* or the giant ripper lizard have been found throughout South Australia, Queensland and New South Wales. It would have been very similar to the Komodo in appearance, having a slightly shorter tail with serrated teeth more widely spaced and more curved than the Komodo. However, *Megalania* was far bigger than the Komodo. Although a complete skeleton has never been found, composite remains provide a total length estimate in excess of twenty feet and an average weight in the region of 1000lbs. Assuming his behaviour was similar to a Komodo, a well satiated *Megalania* may have approached nearly one tonne in weight.

Komodo dragons have no natural predators in their own environment. It is thought that monitors are the closest related lizards to snakes, and Komodos certainly include snakes in their diet. However, will the Komodo get a shock when he meets the snake from South America?

KOMODO DRAGON IN PROFILE

Length	Up to 13 feet
Weight	Up to 550 lbs after a heavy meal
Weaponry	A mouth full of flat, serrated teeth; highly adapted for slicing through flesh. Strong sharp claws and toxic saliva that can deliver death by infection.
Speed	15 mph
Weaknesses	A surprisingly inefficient killer, frequently unable to overpower its intended victim
Profile	Prehistoric monster that lives on a prehistoric island. Don't pat them on the head. They won't be amused.
Human Champ	Evander Holyfield approaches cautiously and lands a straight one-two to the maw of the dragon. Perhaps a little stunned by the bravery of the human champ, there is a momentary delay before the dragon reacts quickly and clamps his jaws around Holyfield's forearm. Despite bleeding profusely, Holyfield turns and runs for his life. The dragon gives chase but can't match Holyfield's pace. Holyfield escapes but succumbs eight hours later to his terribly infectious wound.

SERPENT

Snakes often seem to instill fear into people. A bit like spiders, many people have an irrational fear of them. Perhaps it's their forked tongue or the fact that they have no legs. Maybe it is because we imagine them to be to be wet, slimy and scaly (their skin is actually quite dry to touch). Maybe it is because they can tie themselves in knots. Or maybe the fear is actually a rational one. After all, snakes are perfectly capable of killing humans and do so in reasonable numbers each year.

The snake camp is primarily divided into two: firstly, those that use venom to kill their prey, and secondly, constrictors; those that use their muscle to kill their prey; they literally squeeze their life out of their victim. The first group (the invenomators), by virtue of their weaponry, do not have a requirement to grow to a great size. They inject their venom into their victim and wait for the poison to take effect.

The paralysed victim can then be swallowed whole. Because venomous snakes rarely grow beyond ten feet the prey they tackle is comparatively small. Any humans who are bitten and killed by a venomous snake will not end up as a meal, they are simply too big for the snake to eat. Snakes cannot chew food and must swallow all their meals whole.

The number of venomous snake species in the world are too numerous to discuss and even list here if we are to avoid tedium. However, none of them could truly be called an apex predator in their own environment. Their small size means that they frequently become prey items themselves. Large birds of prey often swoop from the sky only to re-emerge from the long grass with a snake ensconced in their talons. It can use those very talons and its sharp beak to tear the snake to pieces and feed it to its young.

For snakes that form the top of the food chain we really need to turn to the constrictors. Some of the snakes that form the constrictor family grow to truly gigantic proportions and anything wanting to make a meal of a large constrictor would have to be an apex predator in its own right. Furthermore, some constrictors are large enough to make a meal of humans.

Constrictors are split into two broad categories, namely boas and pythons. There are two truly massive constrictors alive today, one coming from each camp. The green anaconda of South America is a member of the boa family.

The reticulated python of South East Asia, funnily enough, belongs to the python family. Boas and pythons do not reproduce in the same way. Boas bear live young, whereas pythons lay eggs. Pythons are also among the small number of snakes that show parental care, the female coiling around the clutch of eggs during the two to three months incubation period to protect them from predators.

Constricting snakes are often referred to as being relatively primitive. Their skulls are heavier and their jaws more rigid than other types of snake. They have also retained several anatomical features from the limbed animals from which they are descended.

These include a pelvic girdle and in most species, the remains of back limbs in the form of small claws or spurs. All species have two functioning lungs and several species of boas have heat-sensitive pits in the scales bordering their mouths, which they use to locate prey in the dark.

When both of our snake kings select their prey, they will throw one or more of their coils around the body of the victim. Each time the victim breathes out the snake tightens its grip. Rather than being crushed, the victim eventually dies by suffocation, either because it cannot draw breath or because its heart cannot pump blood.

Once the prey is dead the snake will loosen its hold and search for the head. It swallows this end first gradually releasing the rest of the body from its coils. Constriction is particularly efficient for killing mammals because being warm-blooded, they have to breathe relatively frequently.

A substantial meal can sustain a large snake for several weeks or even months. Anacondas have an impressive list of prey items ranging from wading birds and deer up to fully grown caimans and jaguars. Although, the caiman cannot boast to be the most impressive of the crocodilian family it can grow to about eight feet in length and perhaps because they share the anacondas' habitat, they become common prey items.

The old adage about the female of the species being more deadly than the male rings true again in this case. Female anacondas grow larger than their male counterparts.

Perhaps due to their great size and weight, anacondas spend most of their life submerged in shallow water and usually ambush their prey in the shallows. They favour areas with thick waterside vegetation where they can move unhindered and unseen. With its eyes and nostrils on top if its head, the anaconda can both breathe and view its prey while its stocky body remains submerged under water. It utilizes its powerful jaws to clench onto its prey before it begins the constriction.

Not to be outdone, the reticulated python also has an impressive prey list. It too can swim well, but spends more time on land than in water, seldom straying too far from its den. Birds and mammals such as goats form the majority of its diet, although it has been claimed that they have killed things as large as a horse. When it comes to the crunch, however, which snake is more impressive?

This is a difficult one to answer. It is frequently claimed that the reticulated python is the longest snake in the world, whereas the green anaconda is the heaviest in the world - bulkier and heavier by virtue of its water-bound existence. However, the upper length limit of both snakes is cited in most literature as around 10m or 33 feet.

A snake this large has never been authenticated for either species. Since the early part of the last century the New York Zoological Society has offered a reward of $50,000 to anybody who could bring to them alive, a snake of any species that exceeds 30 feet in length. Although many have searched for this giant specimen it has remained elusive.

Numerous sightings and claims have been made to exceed this figure. In 2004 it was claimed that a 49-foot python had been caught alive and well in the Sumatran jungles. It was subsequently transported to a Javanese zoo where it was eventually measured to be twenty-three feet. Still a big snake, but not quite mythical. The late famous explorer Percy Fawcett famously claimed to have sighted and killed an enormous anaconda during his South American explorations in 1907. Its length was allegedly 62 feet.

Our trusty *Guinness Book of Records* states that the record length for a reticulated python is 32 feet, nine inches for a specimen shot in Celebes, Indonesia in 1912. However, quite how that length was verified remains unclear. It also states that the largest snake ever held in captivity was a reticulated python called Colossus, measuring an impressive twenty-eight feet, six inches and weighing in at 320lbs at her heaviest. By way of comparison, our trusty book claims that the longest anaconda ever measured was a female shot in Brazil in 1960. The claimed length was twenty-seven feet, nine inches and it had a girth of 44 inches. Although not weighed, it was estimated that it exceeded 500lbs.

In the great tradition started by *Jaws*, our two giant snakes have both been the titles of popularist films. *Anaconda* was perhaps a little more successful than *Python* with a better known cast. Although both films essentially had the same simple plot – 40-foot snakes go on the rampage and begin devouring people as they stand on the decks of their river boats – the link to reality is non-existent. Firstly, the anaconda looked more like 60 feet to this observer and despite its enormous bulk it moved with the speed of a black mamba on steroids. The notion that it could pluck people from their boats was comical, as was the suggestion that it would come back for another couple shortly afterwards.

In reality, a large snake would easily be capable of killing a man if it got hold of him. Although capable of explosive strikes, large constrictors are quite slow moving. Furthermore, it would have to be an enormous snake to actually be able to devour a man. In order to get the jaws around the shoulders of even an average-sized man, it would require a truly massive specimen. Swallowing your prey whole can have its limitations. The anaconda can swallow prey much bigger than the size of its mouth since its jaw can unhinge and the jaw bones are only loosely connected to the skull. While the snake eats, its muscles have wave-like contractions, which in turn crush the prey even further as it surges down the gullet. The snake, however, is then left in quite a vulnerable state. After consuming a large meal, constrictors become very slow and lethargic as much of their energy is directed towards digesting their meal.

Not too long ago I watched a documentary on the Discovery channel whereby Mark O'Shea - a British man with a bushy red beard - went off to Venezuela to search for giant anacondas. He would spy an anaconda and just dive into the murky lakes and begin wrestling with a very large snake (and when he got bored he wrestled caimans too), eventually wrapping it around his shoulders so he could weigh it on his portable scales! During his time in Venezuela he caught and catalogued numerous anacondas and a struggle was caught on film where he wrestled an 18-footer, successfully hoisting it from its muddy retreat for weighing (150lbs). He also dragged another anaconda from its lakeside resting place, pointing out how the bulge emanating from its body was the shape of a recently devoured caiman.

The documentary mentioned that Mark O'Shea worked at West Midlands Safari Park by day. Thus, the very next weekend I took a drive up to West Midlands Safari Park to see if he still worked there. I am delighted to say at that time he still did (then he got his own TV series so I don't know if he still does) and was available for me to interrogate. Mark was adamant that 30-foot-plus anacondas do exist and he added that at that size even he would have to think twice before diving in and wrestling one!

He also stated that they were so well camouflaged against the water that frequently he would catch sight of a large snake, which had obviously been there for minutes before he had even noticed it. His point was that there are so many large anacondas there that you will just never find, even if you are looking for them. It stands to reason, therefore, that there are larger snakes out there than we have so far caught. Also, he pointed out that they sighted some rather large snake trails in the mud besides the lakes, suggesting the existence of very large snakes, much bigger than those he caught.

Curiously, snakes appear to have altered very little in their evolution. Bone fragments discovered of large prehistoric snakes seem to suggest sizes only slightly larger than today's big constrictors. Indeed, at around 45 feet in length, many experts would suggest they were no larger than today's largest anacondas and reticulated pythons.

Of the two giant constrictors, it is the anaconda that is perhaps the slightly more impressive. Although the reticulated python may reach a greater length, by virtue of it being a ground snake, it is far lighter and upper weight limits put it at no more than 400lbs, even for a snake exceeding 30 feet.

Anacondas on the other hand are only slightly shorter but with the water supporting their vast bulk, they are far heavier.

A specimen exceeding 30 feet should comfortably reach 500lbs, probably more. Also, their regular prey items are perhaps slightly impressive. A snake that can kill and eat medium-sized crocodilians as well as large cats has to be respected. For this reason it is the anaconda that will represent the snakes against the Komodo dragon.

GREEN ANACONDA

Length	30 foot +
Weight	600lbs +
Weaponry	600lbs of solid muscular coils ready to squeeze the life out of potential victims!
Speed	On land – less than 1mph In water – 5mph
Weaknesses	On land extremely vulnerable
Profile	A prehistoric creature of nightmares that crushes you then eats you whole. Nice.
Human Champ	Unaccustomed to punching so low Evander Holyfield approaches the water's edge with extreme caution. This proves his undoing as the 600lb-er launches at him and locks onto his leg with surprising speed. The snake begins to coil around the boxing champ and succeeds in dragging him from his feet and into deeper water. Evander is drowned after struggling bravely for just over four minutes.

BIG FIGHT BUILD UP

This is proving a very difficult one to call with the experts. Both predators live in very different environments and neither has had to be particularly adaptable over the years. They are both living dinosaurs and some of our experts are calling their predatory habits dinosaurian – that is to say, outdated.

This view may seem a little unfair on our protagonists. The Komodo dragon has after all adapted successfully to a harsh environment where all other large predators have failed to carve out an existence. Surely then it deserves its place at the top of the food chain? The question that everybody is asking is how it will cope when it comes face to face with a predator of similar stature? Will it crumble in the wake of competition or rise to the challenge?

The anaconda perhaps commands more respect from the betting community. It is not the only large predator within the confines of the South American swamps. Large jungle cats and small crocodilians vie with the anaconda for the title of apex predator. However, the anaconda has demonstrated a willingness to feed on adult specimens of both creatures. It has no natural enemies as an adult so why would our experts be sceptical?

The fact is that both of our dinosaurian protagonists are not without their weaknesses. They are both cold-blooded and susceptible to a rapid burn out. The anaconda particularly is very vulnerable when out of its watery habitat, reduced to a crawl when trying to move its huge bulk around. The Komodo by contrast is comfortable in the water and is obviously very dangerous when on land.

Yet the Komodo is a surprisingly inefficient hunter, rarely bagging its catch on the first attempt. If it didn't have the benefit of the bacterial weapon it would often go very hungry and may even starve. The anaconda by contrast is a much more efficient hunter. Once it has a hold of its prey, little escapes.

As always, everything probably rests on who makes the first successful strike. The Komodo will possess greater mobility, with a larger array of weaponry. The anaconda on the other hand is more focused in the weaponry department with a more lethal result if it can unleash its potential. However, deprived of the potential to ambush its quarry, its predatory potential does decrease. Mobility is the anaconda's key weakness and the Komodo may well be able to exploit this.

All in all this fight is looking like a fairly even bet, with the big snake perhaps entering as a slight favourite. Assuming that both protagonists are well fed, they will enter at a similar weight and both possess the potential to kill the other. It's going to be another close, fascinating match-up.

SECONDS OUT

For much of the introductions the 30-foot snake seems to struggle as it backs off the beach and retreats into the swampy water beside the sand. The Komodo flicks out its forked tongue 'tasting the scene', not quite sure what to make of the giant snake. Similarly, the anaconda looks wary, unsure what to make of the giant lizard before it.

The anaconda is nearly wholly in the water when the dragon begins to advance. This prompts the snake to rear up its head and make a loud hissing sound, a clear warning to the Komodo of what to expect should it advance further. The big lizard heeds the warning and backs off, allowing the snake to complete its retreat into the water.

The snake remains motionless at the water's edge, its head barely visible and its huge body now totally hidden thanks to the murky water. A big surprise awaits the unwary, but the Komodo remains fully aware of the hidden danger lurking just off-shore.

Suddenly it is as if the dragon just loses patience with this cat and mouse game. He lurches swamp-wards at top speed intent on a direct attack on the anaconda. She is prepared for such an eventuality, however, and as the Komodo approaches she launches her counter attack with surprising speed. The anaconda's head darts forward, it mouth opens wide and as the hapless dragon blindly advances, the anaconda sinks her teeth into his shoulder.

The dragon reacts wildly to the snake bite, lurches this way and that in an attempt to shed this large parasite, but the anaconda's grip holds and furthermore, it begins to coil around the neck and middle of the Komodo. Our dragon continues in its attempt to unravel itself, managing to dig its claws into the flesh of the snake and also managing to bite into the enveloping coils, albeit a weak bite. As the coils tighten around the neck of the dragon its ability to move and therefore fight back becomes severely restricted. It manages to claw and bite a little more, before the snake becomes all-encompassing and as the dragon struggles, the bleeding snake just seems to further tighten its grip. The dragon slowly stops its struggling and with each breath it draws, the vice-like grip around its middle squeezes just a little bit harder. It is several more minutes before the dragon suffocates and the anaconda releases its coils from around the victim.

The anaconda finds the head of the dragon and unhinges its jaws and begins the process of swallowing its prey. It swallows the head before realising that even she will be unable to devour something as large as this Komodo dragon. She slinks off into the swamp to nurse her injuries of battle.

The dragon may be dead, but he will have his revenge. Twice he managed to bite the snake and pierce the skin. His virulent bacteria immediately set about the process of creating infection. The anaconda may have won the battle, but she will ultimately lose the war. Within 48 hours the infection will spread and the anaconda will also die. Even in death the Komodo proves deadly. At best he earned an honourable draw; at worst he went down to a points defeat.

Chapter 7
Miscellaneous
Predators

Throughout this book we have largely been discussing theoretical match-ups along a specific theme, the winner of each bout gaining a title befitting the victory. That is, current Daddy of the oceans, current Daddy on land, all time-historical claimant on both land and in the oceans, clash of the living dinosaurs, etc. We have dealt exclusively with animals that are or were at one time active predators. That is to say, they aggressively hunt other animals for food and are therefore used to killing for a living. Aggressive behaviour is their accepted behaviour. We could continue creating fascinating match-ups *ad infinitum* and describing each clash in detail, but the intention is not to be exhaustive. However, there are some key areas of popular fascination and many unanswered questions that have not been tackled by the chapters so far. Therefore, in this final chapter we will discuss some loose ends and frequently asked questions.

DOGS

The first of these relates to the area of dogs and the top fighting breed. When I was young (pre-teen) my dad came home one day with a Rottweiler puppy. Jasper became the centre of my world as I cared and nurtured him, took him for walks, etc. He grew into a big strong dog whose fondness of people was legendary. To my constant dismay, however, his strong alpha male instincts led him to want to fight with every other dog he came across that didn't back down to his nasty stares. Over the years I had my share of hair-raising encounters when strange dogs would come bounding up (unleashed) and Jasper (leashed) would attempt to eat the other dog who would typically attempt the same. I had little to fear for Jasper, except when he once clashed with another Rottweiler. He was simply too big and strong for the dogs we usually encountered. Big mongrels, Great Danes, German shepherds, boxers; all of them picked fights with Jasper over the years, but none ever came close to looking like they could hurt him. I wouldn't say the same the other way around. Being in the middle of a dog fight is not a pleasant experience, particularly as you try and hold your dog back with one hand and fight the other dog off with your free hand !

Yet despite what I have said and despite the fear many people exhibited at Jasper's appearance (100lbs of solid muscle and a representative of the devil-dog species straight out of the *Omen* films), he was no fighting dog. He was highly protective of family members and an excellent guard dog when left alone in the house, but he was no trained killer. When strangers were welcomed into the house he would "lick them to death" instead of biting their leg off! He may have been a wolf in our living room, but he was fed his dinner everyday and never had to hunt to eat. He never had to kill to feed and was thoroughly domesticated. He didn't have a true killer instinct. If pitched against a true fighting dog or a large wild wolf he wouldn't have stood a chance. But what if he had been born into the wild or trained from birth to fight? Would a large Rottweiler be the Daddy doggy or does that title belong to another pooch?

For those of us who see our dogs as part of the family and not a vicious killer, it is difficult to believe that a subculture of people raise and keep dogs for the purpose of using them as gambling tools in fighting pits. However, this was certainly the case historically and continues unabaited (albeit illegally) today. There can be no denying that the use of bulldogs throughout the past couple of thousand years as hunters of rough, large game, controllers of bulls and as gambling tools against bulls, bears, badgers and their own kind, has shaped the dog into the breed we know today. But the use of the bulldog exclusively for *dog-fighting* is a modern development, which came about when bull-baiting was outlawed in the 1800's. Yes, we are referring to the modern day British bulldog. A short, squat breed that usually weighs about 60lbs and often doesn't like to take exercise was used to bait a wide array of large animals (its name comes from its bull-baiting origins) and then pitted against each other often in fights to the death.

The baiting of large fierce animals such as bears or bulls was historically considered fit entertainment for royalty while the fighting of dog against dog was looked upon as a 'poor relation' to the baiting of larger, more powerful animals. As long as there are men with no regard for society's laws seeking to prove the prowess of their dogs, there will be dog fighting. While animal fighting occurs almost everywhere in the world, dog fighting and fighting dogs have historically been associated with the United Kingdom. The baiting of bulls by dogs was even at one point *required* by law.

The question must be posed, however, as to whether the modern bulldog is an accurate representation of true bull-baiting dogs? Paintings from the early 1800s of bull-baiting scenes suggest otherwise. One painter who did many such scenes always without exception represented the bulldogs with long straight legs; agile bodies (nothing overdone about it); a full straight tail, in size about 40 to 60 pounds; with deep full muzzles, giving a strong bite. There are no short, deformed noses. There are no bowed legs and fiddle fronts; no weak, wide shoulders; no short tail; no wrinkles on the head.

Why? Because the deformities listed above would all be detrimental to a real baiting dog. Short, bowed legs do only one thing - make a dog less agile. A dog facing a maddened bull must be able to spring about tirelessly, leaping and dodging; things a dog with a weak front cannot do well. A dog with an overly wide chest, legs hung on the 'outside' of the dog (not under it) with weak pasterns and flat feet is simply not an athlete. Neither is an overly large dog; it will have to be less than 80 pounds. Large, heavy dogs lack the wind and agility to survive close contact with a bull. [Note: Australian cattle dogs; a breed that works bulls in the Australian outback to this day; are small, 35lb dogs. Large dogs simply cannot do the work.] Sadly, whilst being cute and roly poly, the short, bow-legged, heavy bodied, heavy headed, short muzzled dogs marketed today as "recreated baiting bulldogs" are in all likelihood no less a fancy of an overactive imagination.

Are original bulldogs extinct? If they are, why would dogs identical in appearance to baiting dogs still exist today? Many of the pictures drawn from the time could easily meet the standard of the today's American pit bull terrier. In essence that probably answers the question. Through breeding, the dogs have probably diversified into several different types, from large mastiff-like bulldogs used primarily as guardians, to tiny fighting dogs, to the modern pug-faced bulldog. The original bull baiter is unlikely to have been today's British bulldog but instead a distant relative. It is much more likely that the original bull baiter was an American pit bull or a breed perhaps now extinct that was a very close relative.

There can be no doubt that certain dog breeds are tremendous hunters. When in packs dogs are capable of bringing down much larger quarry. African hunting dogs and wolves are classic examples of wild dogs doing just this. Dogs have been used through the ages to hunt everything from bulls to tigers very successfully. However, whenever organisms fight, size usually wins the day. An excellent featherweight will have little chance even against the most mediocre of heavyweights. Thus, when in the singular does an American pit bull weighing in at around 60lbs have a chance against say a Rottweiler weighing in on average at over twice that?

For the reasons discussed above the answer is probably yes. American pit bulls are definitely the athletes of the dog world. They can leap and bound around effortlessly, seeming not to tire. They have amazing jaw strength; once they have seized onto their victim, it is possible to lift them clean off the ground and their grip will still hold even as they are swung around.

A fictional account of this sort of clash was documented in the classic book *White Fang* by Jack London. White Fang was a dog that became a pit-fighting sensation, dispatching every dog put before him. One day a short, squat pit bull/bulldog type entered the arena. Despite this dog bleeding profusely it refused to give in and eventually got a tenuous grip on White Fang. It just wouldn't leg go and nothing White Fang could do would loosen its grip. Eventually the grip inched ever upwards towards the throat of White Fang.

Although a fictional account it probably has a ring of truth to it. Dog fights were common at the time the book was written and the author probably drew on real experiences or accounts of them. A Rottweiler is a large, heavy-boned dog, but it isn't the largest. It is still reasonably manoeuvrable when compared to some breeds and has a particularly strong bite when compared to say a German shepherd of the same size. It is reported that the Romans used the Rottweiler as a dog of war 2000 years ago, although the modern breed is more suited to cattle herding. Thus, if a Rottweiler were pitched against an American pit bull it is quite possible that the Rottweiler may be able to use its size and weight to 'maul' the smaller dog in the early stages. However, the American pitbull was bred to fight. It would more than likely be able to evade the attacks of the bigger dog and even absorb any successful attacks from the Rottweiler. Pitbulls are noted for their high pain tolerance. Soon the big dog would tire and then the pitbull would probably come into its own. Pitbulls are known to frequently go for the throats when they meet a strange dog. This just serves to demonstrate their instinctive breeding and nature. A Rottweiler simply won't possess this instinct and as a result the pitbull would always start as favourite.

However, we mentioned that there are still larger dogs. They don't really come any bigger or heavier than the Old English mastiff. Indeed, this is one of the oldest breeds and probably the one from which the likes of the Rottweiler and the pit bull owe some of their lineage. These dogs are so large that somebody once said that 'as is a lion to a cat, so is a mastiff compared to a dog'. Mastiffs are massive, powerful and muscular, commonly exceeding over 200lbs in weight with the average weight around about 180lbs for an adult male. The largest ever healthy mastiff weighed an impressive 330lbs and the dog was not overweight. This dog was so massive that it was actually approaching the size and weight of an adult lion. Mastiffs were initially valued as fierce guard and fighting dogs and let's face it, who would argue with a dog nearly as big as a lion? The Romans also used them as arena fighting dogs.

There are a few other breeds that have been bred specifically for fighting, most listing the Old English mastiff as an ancestor. The English Dangerous Dogs Act of 1991 actually banned three species of dog but interestingly, the American pit bull was spared provided the owners adhered to strict restrictions, including registering, neutering and microchipping the dog. The other three species were the Dogo Argentino (Argentinian mastiff), the Fila Brazileiro (Brazilian mastiff) and the Japanese Tosa.

The Argentine mastiff weighs in between 80 and 100lbs and was bred initially to be a big game-hunting dog and loyal family guardian. Dr Antonio Nores Martinez created the breed by mixing various lineages and eventually created a bullish and fearless hunter with great stamina. Unfortunately, the breed instantly appealed to those that organise and enjoy dogfights, giving it a bad reputation amongst many quarters.

The Brazilian mastiff is a little heavier than the Argentine, weighing in between 90 and 110lbs. The reason they are banned in Britain is probably more down to their temperament than their fighting ability. The Fila Brazileiro has an inherent distrust of strangers and many breeders express the opinion that Filas simply cannot be socialised to like people. They routinely attack strangers.

The final banned dog, the Japanese Tosa, has a fearsome fighting reputation. The western breed is also massive and can commonly weigh as much as 200lbs, with 150lbs + being the average. They are bold and fearless dogs and have a very high pain tolerance due to their fighting origins. Japanese dog-fighting rules were perhaps slightly more civil than their western equivalents as rarely did dogs die or become seriously injured from their encounters. Tosas are instinctively aggressive towards other dogs (which is not good for the other dog). Around the early 1800s the best of the original Japanese Tosas were bred with the newly imported European breeds such as the mastiff to increase their size. The result was a powerful, agile and surprisingly athletic mastiff-type dog. This massive dog also excels at weight pulling. The Tosa is a rare breed, even in its native land (where it is bred smaller).

If any dog can give the pit bull a run for its money, it is probably the Japanese Tosa. Its combination of massive size and strength combined with a high level of agility and athleticism make it a dog to be feared, even by pit bulls. If the information that is available on dog fighting is to be believed, these two breeds stand out as the two most dominant fighting dogs and although various breeds have been matched against them, they nearly always come out on top. When pitched against each other the results have apparently been mixed and varied with both breeds having a mixture of success and failure.

At this point I would like to say that dogfighting is a revolting and distasteful practice, and that the only reason that the publishers or I have included it in this book is for the sake of completeness, and the mere thought that anyone might read this section and think that I am endorsing this cruel and barbaric passtime, is abhorrent to both me and to CFZ Press.

SALTWATER CROCODILE

The estuarine or saltwater crocodile is the largest of all the crocodilians alive today. Within the confines of this book you may have thought it to have been conspicuous by its absence so far. The presence of *Deinosuchus* amongst these pages has meant that the crocodilians have been represented in the overall title race by their biggest, nastiest ever representative. However, today's largest croc is simultaneously a living relict from the age of the dinosaurs and arguably the most dangerous predator both in the oceans and on land. How then would he fare in these various categories?

In all likelihood, the saltwater or indo-pacific crocodile would be a major contender in all of the afore-mentioned categories. Crocodilians have changed little in the last 65 million years. Crocodiles are semi-aquatic predators and the saltwater crocodile, as its name implies, is equally at home in the ocean as it is in freshwater. It has legs strong enough to lift its body clear of the ground and as a result is very comfortable on land.

As typical crocodilians the 'saltie' will eat a mixture of live prey and carrion. They use various techniques when hunting but the most common is to lie in wait at the edges of rivers or lakes, waiting for mammals to come within range to drink or cross. Another method is to drift towards prey, using stealth and thereby hoping to catch it off guard. Like all crocodilians the Saltie is unable to chew. Small prey can be swallowed whole, but they must dismember larger prey by spinning violently about their own axis whilst underwater, holding part of the carcass in their jaws and eventually tearing off chunks of flesh for swallowing. Having killed a large prey item, the crocodile will often store its prey in an underwater larder (such as under a rock) to rot. This makes it easier to dismember later.

Saltwater crocodiles feed on a large variety of prey including mammals, birds and fish. They present a real threat to humans and have been responsible for many fatalities. The saltie is prevalent throughout much of northern Australasia and parts of southeast Asia, eating pretty much what it can get its teeth around. Large adults have been known to take down buffalo.

Furthermore, adults can grow very large indeed. It used to be thought that crocodiles would grow indefinitely until they died, hence producing very large, very old crocodiles. However, there is some doubt over this now, and it is likely that maximum size is instead influenced by genetic factors and environmental cues such as temperature, food intake and even incubation temperature. A few individuals seem predisposed towards very large sizes if all the conditions are right. In saltwater crocodiles the average maximum size for males is around fifteen to sixteen feet. It is extremely unusual to find individuals larger than this – twenty-footers are a rarity indeed, and only a small handful of individuals have ever been recorded at, or over, this length.

In all species of crocodilians the men outgrow the ladies. In saltwater crocodiles males can be twice the length of females, whereas in Nile crocodiles males may only be 30% larger than females. In many crocodile species males also grow *faster* than females but in some, e.g. American alligators, females outgrow males for the first few months before being overtaken.

So how big do salties actually get? Like all other species in this book they are responsible for a few 'big fish stories'; one of the largest saltwater crocodiles ever reported was a massive 10.1m (33.1 feet)! This animal was apparently killed in the Bay of Bengal, and was so large only its head was recovered. A skull reportedly belonging to this animal was stored in the British Museum, but when it was later measured it was estimated to have come from a sixteen-foot crocodile – less than half the claimed length.

The skull of another supposed monster (this time twenty-nine feet long) was also later determined to belong to a crocodile no larger than sixteen feet. This is still a big crocodile but typical of the exaggeration we have come to associate with large specimens. Still, some of these stories seem more credible. Saltwater crocodiles above twenty feet in length were certainly much more common in Australia and S.E. Asia before extensive hunting for their skins in the 1940s, 50s and 60s wiped out many of the big crocodiles. Some old hunters claim to have shot animals over twenty-six feet during this period (e.g. a twenty-seven-foot saltwater crocodile from the Staaten River in Queensland in the early 1970s). But without reliable measurements such record claims are lost to the past.

So what is the largest crocodile ever reliably recorded? In more recent times there have been very few reliable measurements of extremely large crocodiles but they *do* exist. A skull from a saltwater crocodile from Orissa, India, was large enough to have come from a crocodile between twenty and twenty-three feet in length. Its true size remains a mystery. The two largest reliable records of complete animals are both from twenty-foot crocodiles: the first was shot in the Mary River in the Northern Territory of Australia in 1974 by poachers and measured by wildlife rangers; the second was killed in 1983 in the Fly River in Papua New Guinea. In this latter crocodile it was actually the skin that was measured by zoologist Jerome Montague and as skins are known to underestimate the size of the actual animal it's likely this crocodile was at least another four inches longer. Unfortunately, because of the time needed for wild crocodiles to reach this size, the low number of individuals, which seem predisposed to reach such sizes and problems of crocodiles conflicting with expanding human populations, it seems unlikely that we will see many of these giants again in the immediate future.

A typical-sized saltwater crocodile in the region of fourteen to fifteen feet in length will balance the scales at around 500kg in weight. However, as we have already mentioned in a previous chapter, crocodiles increase massively in girth with increased length and by the time eighteen feet is reached individuals usually exceed a tonne in weight. It seems likely that any specimens exceeding twenty-three feet in length will possibly exceed two tonnes in weight.

In the light of this information, how will the saltwater crocodile perform in our various categories? Firstly, dealing with the arena of "living dinosaurs", it is larger than both the anaconda and the Komodo dragon combined. Although the snake may be longer in total length, even a 30-foot + anaconda could seem relatively slim when next to even a twenty-foot crocodile. The

---

According to *Crocodiles: Their natural history, folklore and conservation* by C.A.W Guggisberg, a specimen was shot on the MacArthur bank of the Norman River in Queensland, Australia in 1957, measured 28ft 4in. It was shot by Mrs Kris Powloski and measured by her husband Ron who was a recognised crocodile expert who set up some of the first crocodile farms in Australia.

Komodo dragon would probably lack the bite strength to pierce the armour plating on the crocodile's back and would also be heavily outweighed. Although both the Komodo dragon and the anaconda are predators to be feared in their own right, it is hard to see them defeating a large saltwater crocodile. All three "living dinosaurs" share similar traits. Their reptilian nature makes them all appear ugly and frightening to us. Despite their impressive size, in my opinion they are all surprisingly inefficient killers. They lack the ability to chew and must swallow prey (or lumps of them) as a whole. They are all cold-blooded and have the propensity to tire quickly in the event of a long struggle, although it must be said that there are a few cases on record where large crocodiles have subdued and killed rhinos and hippos after a long struggle. The crocodile probably has the thickest skin and therefore the best defence against the others. Combine this with its immense weight and size and it should probably emerge as an easy victor against either the dragon or the snake.

What about when the crocodile ventures into the sea: does it have anything to fear there? The classic encounter that is often postulated is the scenario where a saltwater crocodile meets a great white shark. Both beasties grow to similar lengths although the shark, being purely water-borne, has a greater girth and is possibly a little heavier. Most commentators on such a clash usually favour the shark to come out on top in its natural environment (the crocodile only being semi adapted to life in the oceans). Personally, I find it hard to argue against such an outcome. The crocodile may have thick scales upon its back but it has a soft underbelly; exactly the area the shark would most likely attack. The shark's teeth are made for ripping even the toughest of hides, and probably as the heavier combatant it would be hard to fight back against it.

A cryptozoologist friend of mine, and author on the subject of large crocodiles, argues vehemently against this view. From his standpoint large crocodiles are all-conquering behemoths that sweep all before them and woe betide most creatures that should stand in their way. His argument lies heavily on the bite strength of the crocodile. The muscles that open their jaws are very weak, but the muscles that bite down onto prey are *very* strong. The bite pressure of the crocodile is legendary and can be likened to a metal vice clamping down on a hapless victim. Its teeth may not be made for slicing through prey, but the vice-like bite of a crocodile can easily crush bones. It is often claimed that they can even crush the leg bones of very large animals such as hippos. My friend would argue that this massive bite would prove too damaging to most creatures the crocodile strikes. Indeed, he told me that there have been reports of huge Nile crocodiles (only slightly smaller than saltwater crocs) attacking adult elephants and preying frequently on adult lions. I once remember attending one of his talks where he stated that a large crocodile would make mincemeat of a great white.

I once sat down with him and suggested the possibility of a saltwater crocodile going head to head with a polar bear. His response was that the crocodile drags the bear into deep water and eats it. I pointed out that the bear was capable of bringing down very large prey, including its remarkable habit of fishing for whales. However, he was having none of it. In his eyes the crocodile was capable of bringing down anything but the very largest land animals.

His argument, whilst in my opinion overly balanced in favour of the crocodile, has some merit. A very large saltwater crocodile will outweigh even the largest polar bear. However, the average weights of the saltwater crocodile and the polar bear are not too dissimilar to each other at around 400-500kg. Nile crocodiles have certainly been known to prey on adult lions, ambushing them at waterholes. Yet similarly, if they shared the same territory, polar bears would also predate on lions.

Much of the predatory success of the crocodile is down to its element of surprise. As already mentioned I believe that it is a surprisingly inefficient killer. Its only real weaponry comes from those gaping jaws and they become less effectual if the intended prey knows of its presence. A lion, for example, would fight back if it knew it was under attack. Often, however, the crocodile will strike before the lion knows it is under attack, thereby gaining a crucial advantage. The polar bear, however, would walk through any lion counter-attack as if it didn't exist.

Crocodiles also lack mobility on land. They are capable of short bursts of speed, but are not capable of sharp turns and have difficulty in wielding those jaws to their advantage. A piece of footage floating about the internet shows a tiger attacking and killing quite a large crocodile that it ambushes. It jumps on top of its back and attacks the skull area. The crocodile is unable to dislodge the big cat and cannot strike with its jaws. The crocodile was quite a bit larger than the cat, which would probably have started as an underdog. If big cats can attack and kill much larger crocodiles, then so probably can large bears, be they polar or brown bears of sufficient size. However, the film was taken during a drought, and so the crocodile (which seemed very sluggish) was probably suffering from heat exhaustion.

The crocodile is an excellent predator and a true evolutionary success story, but it is difficult to make a case for the crocodile against today's top marine predators. Also, despite a clear weight advantage over the polar bear, it would struggle to make that advantage count. It is less manoeuvrable than the bear and its weaponry, although more devastating if it strikes, is less likely to do it successfully. It is just as easy to see the bear smashing crocodilian skulls as it is to see the crocodile crunching down on bear shins. It's a close one to call, but the crocodile is a major contender if not a champion.

CREEPY CRAWLIES

Much of the inspiration for this book came from a book I once read called *The Red Hourglass* by Gordon Grice. It was a book without true definition and was a mixture of factual natural history and the author's own experiences. Each chapter consisted of abrupt titles such as 'Canid', 'Pig', 'Tarantula', 'Black Widow', 'Brown Recluse Spider', 'Praying Mantis', etc.

The book was immensely interesting to me, but it was the chapters on insects and other invertebrates that really hooked the reader. There is little denying that most people find insects creepy, disturbing and almost alien. Most people will know someone who has a phobia of spiders. These eight-legged aliens frequently invade our homes and I am forever releasing them back into the sanctuary of the garden to stop my 'other half' screaming.

It seems completely illogical that we should be frightened of something so small. Even some of the miniature relatives of tarantulas I dispatch back into the English countryside are less than a thousandth of my size. Yet some creepy crawlies are dangerous to humans due to their venom. Grice dealt with several of these creatures in his book and although I'm not sure he intended it, he created a sort of insect deathmatch arena. By catching various different insects near his home, he would often put them into the same tanks to see how they got on. Invariably they failed to bond and make a lasting friendship. In fact, the tank was usually only big enough for one of them....

Many species of spider are potentially deadly to humans. The male Sydney funnel web is typically rated as the most dangerous spider in the world. Its venom is particularly nasty and above all this spider is aggressive. It has the habit of crawling into warm, dry places such as a pair of shoes during the night. The victim is typically bitten when they put their shoes on the next morning. They also drop into swimming pools and bite those that dare to step on them as they bask on the pool floor. They can trap a small bubble of air in hairs around the abdomen that can aid both breathing and floating. They have been known to survive for over 24 hours under water. With a body length of over two inches, the funnel web is quite a large spider.

The North American black widow and its relatives (such as the Australian redback) also have a fearsome reputation. They are tiny, owning a body like a large pea. However, they rarely leave their webs, so unless a body part such as a hand is placed directly into the web, the chances of being bitten are small. Furthermore, many bites are ineffective due to the spider's small jaws. However, when it does pierce the skin, the black widow's venom can prove deadly. Widow bite victims have been known to attempt suicide to prevent the terrible pain they suffer. All over body cramps can result and some victims have suffered a heart attack from the pain. Also, the male black widow rarely survives its own mating process and can become the prey even before mating occurs.

The banana spider of South America can also prove deadly. Between 1970 and 1980 more than 7000 people in south-eastern Brazil were admitted to hospital with bites from this spider. Similarly, the brown recluse spider can prove deadly. The venom of this spider can cause severe skin necrosis (rotting of the flesh). The banana spider is often quoted as being the most venomous spider in the world, whereas the funnel web is often quoted as being the most toxic to humans.

The Tarantula on the other hand is something completely different. Some types of Tarantula such as the Goliath South American bird-eating spider can grow up to eleven inches across. The Tarantula lacks fancy weaponry. Its venom is not lethal. Some spiders have evolved complex predatory behaviours, but tarantulas earn their meals the old-fashioned way. They hide until some senseless critter is passing by and pounce on it like a mugger, overcoming it with sheer brute force and a nasty set of mandibles. Tarantulas don't build snares, they don't use tricks and although they possess a modicum of venom it isn't really necessary to subdue their victims. Tarantulas are 'primitive' spiders and like the crocodile, debunk a common myth about evolution; namely that the further evolved animals replace outmoded, unsuccessful ones. Today it prospers around the world from rainforests to desert.

Is the tarantula the Daddy creepy crawly? Well, not exactly; at least not all the time. Arthropods have a habit of preying on each other and the terrain or the circumstances often dictate who will emerge as the victor. For example, black widows and brown recluse spiders regularly prey on each other. Grice, in his 'experiments' wrote of the prowess of a carabid beetle that mashed every creepy crawly he put into its cage with its huge mandibles. However, it met its match in a widow that managed to neutralise its weapons with spider silk before biting it on the antenna. Death soon resulted.

Black widows have been known to routinely knock off much larger predators, but like most animals in the food chain, it sometimes makes a meal for something else. The praying mantis often feeds on widows, but they also make up the prey. Widows are sometimes paralysed by wasps, which in turn use them as live food for their larval young. The innocuous looking daddy longlegs spiders are said to eat widows, a real downer for the widow and its aspirant nature to be the 'Daddy' Still, the webs that widows weave are remarkably strong and if prey becomes entwined the widow can devour large prey. For example, six-inch scorpion husks have been found in widow webs. A widow's most dangerous enemy is often another widow, particularly if you are male.

A large Tarantula would have to start as the favourite against most other creepy crawlies. If something venomous could unleash its toxins on the tarantula then the result would be different, but the primitive mugging method would prove difficult to defeat. If a daddy longlegs can prey on black widows, then the tarantula should have little difficulty. Yet the Tarantula has a nemesis of its own, a predator so specialised that is has evolved purely for the purpose of Tarantula-eating.

The Tarantula is the largest and strongest spider. However, it has a fearsome rival in the largest and strongest kind of wasp; the Tarantula hawk. The feud between these two boneless nasties rivals some of the other dramatic predator rivalries of the animal kingdom. They are as inter-twined as the sperm whale and the giant squid. The Tarantula is a primitive generalist, it takes any prey it can over-power and disable. The Tarantula hawk, however, is far from primitive. It is one of the most specialised predators on earth. Its speciality is hunting Tarantulas. In the wild it is the Tarantula hawk that usually emerges victorious, resulting in a horrible death for the tarantula.

The Tarantula hawk relies on ambush. It needs only to catch the spider by surprise and make a successful sting. With the spider suitably paralysed, the wasp will drag its much larger quarry back to its burrow where it will deposit an egg in the spider's abdomen. A worm-like larva then hatches from that egg and devours the Tarantula from the inside. It takes several weeks to finish the large meal and saves the major organs until last. A dead spider would rot before the larva could hatch, so a mother hawk carefully places the sting to leave the spider alive but paralysed. Spiders removed from wasp burrows have been known to last nine months in this condition!

Yet if a Tarantula hawk is placed in a Tarantula's cage (removing the ambush element), the Tarantula usually makes a meal of the Tarantula hawk. Similarly, they usually do the same in the wild if the hawk attacks without the benefit of an ambush. Those large scimitar fangs make short work of the smaller wasp. The wasp is fast and one of the stronger insects, but it is no match for a mugger in a street fight, particularly one that is often ten times as heavy as it is (the wasp is only a few inches long, including the stinger). The hawk may have its sting, but the Tarantula has a venomous bite. Either one could paralyse the other with one shot.

In essence, there are many dangers in the invertebrate world both to humans and each other. However, it lacks a king of the jungle. No one individual species emerges to truly conquer all others, at least not one that we have so far discovered. There may yet still be something lurking in the jungles. Watch this space….

THE CASE OF THE SABRE-TOOTH AND THE RUNNING BEAR

Our present day big kitties took a bit of a mauling in an earlier chapter. Most people are aware that modern day big cats used to have a relative with very big incisors. As I remember, virtually all my books on dinosaurs from when I was young told me that large sabre-toothed cats were the dominant predator of their era and were capable of taking down the largest herbivores of their day. Supposedly even the woolly mammoth wasn't safe from that amazing set of gnashers. Perhaps then our current crop of big cats has simply mellowed with age? Did the big cats rule a bygone era and how would they have fared today?

The largest sabre-toothed cat so far discovered goes under the name of *Smilodon*. This cat is often referred to as being the size of a lion, with a similarity in form, but being shorter in stature. It had a stubby tail and powerful forequarters adapted to grappling with prey. Its thick muscular neck ended in a relatively large head with a mouth that bore sabres that were seven inches along their outer curvature. People postulated as to exactly what the sabres were for. Theories ranged from using them like ice axes for tree climbing, grubbing for food like walruses, using them to pierce the skull of prey or to prise apart the backbone of prey as some big cats - for example jaguars - do today.

Calculations reveal that whilst the stiletto-like canines of the *Smilodon* could readily skewer flesh, they would shatter on impact with bone. *Smilodon* had a large gape and enormous jaw muscles, but it seems unlikely that they could have powered their sabres through leathery hide and sinew. Nor could the neck muscles have hammered the head down hard enough to stab prey. More than likely *Smilodon* would have used it sabres as blades rather than stilettos, probably butting its lower canines into the prey's flanks or throat to provide a pivot against which the muscles of the head could push down the sabres. As it closed its jaws on prey the sabres would slice backwards and outwards through the hide. This method could have been used to tear open the prey's belly or rip the throat out, severing a rich supply of blood vessels with a minimal risk of the teeth hitting bone. Sabre teeth were probably also useful for cutting and slicing up large corpses.

Smilodon was certainly not fleet of foot. Indeed, it was rather ponderous. However, its powerful hind legs enabled it to leap onto prey from an ambush position and being stocky and strong in the forequarters, it would have enabled it to wrestle with large prey before delivering the killer bite. In fact, recent analysis of *Smilodon* leg bones suggests that it was actually far heavier than a modern day lion. Researchers concluded that it was probably between 1.5 and two times as heavy as a lion. Taking those figures, *Smilodon* weighs in at a hefty 600-800lbs.

This makes it the most formidable cat of all time. It probably outweighed a modern day Siberian tiger and would be much more adept at in-fighting. *Smilodon* was more of a bruiser in battle with the added bonus of extra weaponry. There did exist an extinct rival in the form of a 'marsupial lion' from down under, but that was little larger than a modern day lion. *Smilodon* was king of the cats, but could it really challenge the bear and eat woolly mammoths?

In Texas the ancient den of a fossil sabre-tooth called *Homotherium* was discovered full of the severed leg bones of infant mammoths, probably carried home to sabre-toothed kittens by their mother. This, however, is to say very little. Modern day cats can also prey on young elephants, but they have no chance of preying on a healthy adult. The bones of mammoths and sabre-tooths are often found together at the sites of ancient tar pits. Quite possibly mammoths became trapped in the pits and their distress cries attracted the big cats. With the mammoths unable to properly defend themselves, the cats may have a launched an attack only to succumb to the tar pits' sticky grip themselves. Researchers probably erroneously concluded upon finding the remains together that the giant sabres were evidence of the cats predating on the huge herbivore. In reality, the chances of a *Smilodon* predating on a healthy woolly mammoth were about as likely as a lion bringing down an elephant. To quote Don King, "his chances are slim to none and slim just left town".

Similarly, modern day bears had large extinct relatives. About ten million years ago the bears spawned a new off-shoot that could capitalise on open spaces. These bears moved away from forest omnivory. Known as the great running bears some became giant omnivorous sprinters dispersed across North America. The running bears reached their peak during the Pleistocene era (between 1.8 million and 200,000 years ago). This short-faced bear was rangy, long-limbed, fast moving and very dangerous. It stood approximately five feet at the shoulder and well over double that if it reared up on its hindquarters. It had a short, broad muzzle that would have given it a very powerful bite.

It probably weighed in at a hefty 1500lbs (on average) making it larger than today's average polar bear. The short-faced running bear probably competed directly with big cats for prey. Little is known about their behaviour, but studies of their bone chemistry show that they were predominantly carnivorous. Whether they were predators or scavengers remains a contentious issue. In all likelihood, like nearly all large carnivores, they would have been a mixture of both. The question is one of percentages. Modern theory favours them leaning more towards scavenger than active predator. Their long legs were adapted to ranging far and wide and their powerful bite enabled them to crack open bones to get to the rich marrow inside. As the largest and heaviest active predator of their day, the bears would also probably have bullied other predators off their kills. Effectively they stole kills from smaller predators.

In a similar vein to the large cats, their late Pleistocene extinction probably came about because of the extinction of their large herbivorous prey. Only one running bear lives on today (The South American spectacled bear), albeit in a much modified form. Competition for prey would have been fierce. Apart from big cats, the ancestors of modern day hyenas would also have been a key player. Today's largest hyena, the spotted hyena, weighs in at around 160lbs and is a formidable hunter as well as a scavenger.

In groups they are capable if driving lions off a kill and were it not for their debilitating short back legs they would possibly be a tremendous hunter of large prey in their own right. Run-of-the-mill scavengers lack the ability to crack bones like hyenas.

Hyenas are easily capable of crunching on elephant bones, reducing them to powdered calcium. One of the predecessors to the spotted hyena was called *Pachycrocuta*. *Pachycrocuta* was a 440lb mega scavenger that probably contested kills with sabre-toothed cats much in the same way that today's hyenas and lions contest kills. However, at that size *Pachycrocuta* would probably be more than a match for any modern day cat. Those bone-crushing jaws could prove lethal if it managed to get hold of anything. However, *Smilodon* was likely to have been considerably heavier and this may have proved a problem even to *Pachycrocuta*.

The short-faced running bear also possessed a heavy bite and it was big; very big. In a similar scenario to today's big bears fighting against today's big cats, it is difficult to make a case for *Smilodon* against something as large and dangerous as the short faced running bear. *Smilodon* was a fairly primitive predator. It didn't rely on speed or agility so much. It relied more on its strength, in turn enabling it to unleash the sabres. It is hard to see a scenario where it could out-muscle the running bear or out-manoeuvre it to use its weaponry. Indeed, despite the increased weight and power that *Smilodon* displays compared to modern big cats, the polar bear would probably still have little to fear. The big cats are tremendous predators and pound for pound, they are awesome. However, the sheer size and power displayed by certain members of the bear family remain too much of an obstacle for them to overcome.

DADDY OF THE OCEANS

Sea creatures have featured prominently throughout this book and several clashes of the titans have ensued. Yet an undisputed champion of all time has yet to be formally crowned. The great white shark was defeated by the orca and clearly would be eaten by its larger relative *Carcharodon megalodon*.

The orca may have emerged victorious against the shark and is a truly amazing predator. In packs they have demonstrated that they are capable of hunting down prey much larger than themselves, including the heaviest creature to have ever lived on this fair planet of ours – the blue whale. They have also demonstrated their capabilities to hunt sperm whales, albeit females and juveniles. However, a lone orca would start as a heavy underdog against either a megalodon or a megapli. The orca would be heavily outweighed and outgunned in the weaponry department. It would be extremely hard pressed to make its superior agility and intelligence count in a one-to-one stand-off.

Similarly, today's largest active hunter, the sperm whale is very formidable when the opponent is a large bull male. Pound for pound, the orca probably rates higher than the sperm whale, but the nature of this book is not to discuss the merits of the pound for pound chart. If that were the case we would probably be discussing the capabilities of army ants and piranhas. Instead, we are interested in the facts as they stand before us and the fact remains that an average bull sperm whale outweighs even the largest orca. The largest sperm whale will outweigh the largest orca fivefold and over. The orca possesses greater speed and manoeuvrability and has to be rated as the superior hunter and predator. However, orcas are not known to hunt giant squid. This is perhaps because they don't make deep dives, don't like the taste of large squid and perhaps crucially, the giant squid is a formidable opponent to overcome. That is, the squid would pose more of a threat to an orca than a sperm whale. Ultimately and in isolation, the sperm whale would probably pose a greater threat to the orca than the other way around.

Thus given this assumption the question arises as to how today's top active hunter of large prey would fare against the top predators of the prehistoric seas. Could a sperm whale fight off a megalodon or large pliosaur. The question is obviously one of huge conjecture and it is likely that the whale would start with a size advantage. Even the largest pliosuars and megalodons were unlikely to have reached the record 84 feet claimed for the largest sperm whale. Furthermore, the whale would probably have a weight advantage, particularly over the cartilaginous shark. However, both the shark and the pliosuar begin with a significant advantage in the weaponry department. The teeth of the whale are made for gripping and grasping slippery prey, such as squid, rather than tearing off chunks of flesh. The bite force generated by a 60 to 70-foot pliosaur would be tremendous and the ripping capability of a similarly sized shark would have been frightening. Sperm whales are slow moving creatures, we know this from our observations. We can only guess at the locomotion of our prehistoric predators, and it unlikely that they were speed demons. Yet they were probably capable of short bursts of speed.

In essence, the sperm whale would probably be up against it. Megalodon certainly fed on medium-sized whales and would probably have a successful attack method to launch against large, ponderous mammals. One of the claims that were bounded around when the Monster of Aramberri was first described was that it was probably large and nasty enough to successfully predate on a blue whale if they had lived at the same time. As we have hopefully now demonstrated, you shouldn't believe everything you read in the papers. However, this is not out of the realms of possibility for a 60+ foot pliosaur. If I were a betting man I think I would have to back both megalodon and megapli against a sperm whale. However, I remain uncertain as to who would have eaten who, if the two prehistoric nasties had ever met.

HERBIVOROUS KILLERS

Throughout this book we have delved deep to answer the question of Who's the Daddy? However, we have only dealt with those animals that are active predators; that is to say, carnivorous animals that actively hunt other animals to devour their meat. We have not brought any herbivorous animals into the equation. We have dealt primarily with those creatures that have predated on, or are a direct threat to man; though by doing so a whole group of creatures have been omitted from the survey, many of whom can be very dangerous to both man and other animals.

For example, the silverback gorilla may weigh in excess of 400lbs and could easily beat a man to a pulp, although it is too small to seriously threaten a polar bear and lacks the weaponry to cause severe damage. A fist will nearly always lose out to a claw. The modern gorilla does list a certain *Gigantopithicus* amongst its extinct relatives. *Gigantopithicus* (which was actually more closely related to an orang utan) would have stood nine to ten feet tall if it had stood on its hind legs and have weighed in at as much as 1200lbs. Although believed extinct, some postulate that it lives on as the sasquatch or yeti. An ape that large would probably be able to deter a bear attack. Yet even at that size, the polar bear would probably remain a favourite.

However, much larger herbivores exist than the mountain gorilla. For example, the African hippopotamus is a heavy, aggressive and dangerous animal. It is credited with causing as many human deaths each year as the Nile crocodile. The number of human fatalities from crocodile attacks each year remains largely unknown (many people simply disappear as they go to fetch water). The hippo has a huge gape and massive molars. At over two tonnes in weight it is potentially capable of biting a man in half. Despite living mainly on vegetation, it does have a darker side. When times are harsh, hippos have been known to dine on the flesh of drowned carrion such as wildebeest and zebra, although they are not known to *hunt* these creatures. They have been observed stealing prey (e.g zebra) from Nile crocodiles for their own consumption. The fact that they are capable of muscling Nile crocodiles off their kills is testament to the fighting prowess of the hippo. They are not to be messed with.

Nile crocodiles have sometimes been credited with attacking large prey such as hippos, rhinos and even elephants. A report I once read stated that a large Nile crocodile leapt from the river, grabbing a two-tonne rhino by the nose and slowly managed to drag it under the water and drown it. A similar report described how a Nile crocodile grabbed the leg of an elephant and dragged that to a watery grave. Both stories seem highly unlikely to this author. Juvenile elephants are perhaps under threat from predators, but a healthy adult has little to fear. A pride of starving lions once attacked an adult elephant out of desperation. Their bodies were thrown about everywhere.

When thrown into an arena the modern day African elephant is surely without peer amongst today's land animals. Most of the time the elephant is a gentle giant, feeding harmlessly on plants and trees. However, large bulls enter a state called 'musth' when they are ready to mate and this can have dire consequences for anything stupid or unfortunate enough to stand in their way. Rampaging elephants have been known to flatten entire villages, killing several people.

Furthermore, bull elephants have been known to attack and kill adult rhinoceros in Africa. As dangerous creatures as rhinoceros are, they are no match for an African elephant. It appears that these clashes of herbivorous giants have always occurred when a bull elephant has entered must and could be said to be… well, moody. With those huge tusks and a weight that can exceed seven tonnes, the African elephant needn't fear any predator alive today. Its huge size makes it virtually impregnable to all but man's technology. The big bears had better move on exceed seven tonnes, the African elephant needn't fear any predator alive today. Its huge size makes it virtually impregnable to all but man's technology. The big bears had better move on over.

On land, if today's large herbivores were predatory, they would definitely usurp the likes of the polar bear and the saltwater crocodile. However, the same cannot perhaps be said in the oceans. The largest and heaviest animal to have ever lived, the blue whale, is certainly immune to attack from a single great white shark or killer whale. However, as we have already mentioned, killer whales have been known to attack and kill blue whales when they have hunted in packs. At over 100 feet in total body length, with a weight that can exceed 150 tonnes, the blue whale may be a slow moving plankton feeder, but its sheer size makes it pretty much immune to individual attack. However, it may not have been safe in the prehistoric seas. Both very large pliosaurs and very large megalodons would probably have been capable of launching an attack that could potentially kill a blue whale. The whale may have been able to deploy the use of its tale as a defensive weapon to beat off any would-be assailant, but its defensive weaponry is otherwise notable by its absence. It is quite conceivable that megalodon and megapli could actually attack and eat anything that has ever swum in the oceans of the earth at any time.

Finally, could dinosaurs such as *Tyrannosaurus rex* and *Giganotosaurus* eat anything that has walked on the earth at any time? They would certainly be capable of eating anything that is alive today. The only potential threats would be the tusks of an African elephant that was unwilling to be eaten. However, *T. rex* would most likely outweigh an African elephant with the added bonus of that mouthful of daggers to assist it in taking chunks out of prey. The question that needs to be asked is whether *T. rex* could have fed on the giant herbivores of its own time.

The answer is that unless *T. rex* hunted in packs, it is highly unlikely that it could have taken down the biggest sauropod dinosaurs to have ever walked the earth. Some of the large herbivorous dinosaurs were truly monstrous, making *T. rex* look like a midget. Furthermore, the largest of these were actually longer than a blue whale (although not as heavy).

The largest and heaviest dinosaur for which there is a complete skeleton is *Brachiosaurus*, an enormous giraffe-like dinosaur that stood over 40 feet in height and over seventy feet in length. Its weight was estimated at 40 tonnes. The comparatively light but also essentially complete *Diplodocus* was for a long time credited with being the longest dinosaur. With a long neck and tail this dinosaur stretched to 87 feet and about fifteen tonnes. However, its slender neck may have still left it vulnerable to the bite of large predators.

Yet in recent years the partial bone fragments of much larger dinosaurs have been discovered. The remains of a larger brachiosaur were discovered in the late 1970s. The animal was tentatively named *Ultrasaurus* and was of truly colossal proportions. The creature was estimated to weigh in at a whopping 60 tonnes, exceed 50 feet in height and probably to exceed 100 feet in total length. However, many scientists are of the opinion that *Ultrasaurus* is in fact no such thing and instead represents an outsized *Brachiosaurus*.

Then along came *Seismosaurus*. Although only estimated to weigh about 30 tonnes, *Seismosaurus* is the longest dinosaur so far discovered, with some estimates giving it a total body length in excess of 160 feet! *Seismosaurus* was a diplodicid, i.e. it was closely related to diplodocus. Indeed, in a similar vein to *Ultrasaurus*, many scientists believe that *Seismosaurus* is actually just a large *Diplododocus* and is not a new dinosaur at all.

The title of the biggest dinosaur ever to have lived possibly belongs to a recent discovery that has been christened *Argentinosaurus*, so named after the country in which it was discovered. Some of the backbone vertebrae of this dinosaur measured five feet long by five feet across. It was a truly massive creature and estimated lengths have ranged as high as 130 feet and estimated weights as high as 100 tonnes!

As we have demonstrated already in previous chapters, when bone fragments are the only thing to go on, length and weight measurements are often exaggerated to facilitate extra funding. However, these new discoveries are truly massive creatures and there seems little doubt that the blue whale has been usurped as the longest ever creature to stalk the earth (or sea). Furthermore, although 100 tonnes seems unlikely, there is probably little doubt that some of these dinosaurs did at least exceed half that amount (over ten African bull elephants). Assuming that a *T. rex* could lumber up to an *Argentinosaurus* (they never actually met), it would be heavily outweighed and would face a daunting opponent. It would be comparable to a polar bear facing an African elephant.

Yet *T. rex* would probably fare better against the large sauropods than the polar bear would against an elephant. For a start, these giant sauropods would most likely have been ponderously slow in their movement. Given their sheer size, its seems probable that their nervous systems would have been slow to react to various stimuli. It was once thought that the giant sauropods held their head high in the sky and plucked leaves from high branches. However, palaeontologists now think that these giants actually held their heads lower to the ground. If they held their heads high, their hearts may have not been able to pump sufficient blood to their brains! If they held their heads low, this in turn would have made their relatively slender necks vulnerable to the bite of large theropods such as *T. rex* and *Giganotosaurus*, who could potentially have launched rapid ambush attacks.

Furthermore, although palaeontologists have abandoned the theory that the giant sauropods spent much of their time buoyed up by water, on land they certainly would have lacked dynamism. Also, unlike elephants, sauropods lacked weaponry in the form of tusks. The most likely scenario is that they could have used their tails like heavy whips to dissuade potential predators from making attacks. They may also have been able to rear up onto their back legs and make themselves seem even bigger and menacing.

So little is actually known about the behaviour of dinosaurs and we can but speculate on our various scenarios. *T. rex* emerged as our predatory land champion. Yet at seven tonnes it would appear too small and light to successfully kill and eat an adult *Seisomosaurus*, for example. However, there are enough chinks in the armour of the big sauropods to believe that anything was possible.

Conclusive Summary

Throughout this book we have dealt with large and dangerous animals that fit a variety of categories. However, the subject matter has been far from exhaustive. Many dinosaurs still remain buried in the rocks awaiting discovery. The reign of T. rex and his various rivals, such as *Giganatosaurus*, vying for the top predatory crown, may be short lived. An even bigger nasty may soon be chipped out of the rock. The same applies to *Argentinosaurus*, megalodon, *Liopleurodon* and their ilk. Bigger discoveries are possibly just around the corner.

Also, we have arguably explored space more than we have explored the oceans. The fact that a massive creature such as the giant squid can remain undetected and unknown for so long says volumes about how little we know about the underwater domains in our oceans. Similarly, the fifteen-foot+ megamouth shark is another very recent discovery. Therefore, it is possible that a very large predator may still be waiting to be discovered in the deep blue seas. Although less likely, the same could be said on land. There are still parts of our globe that are largely unexplored. Although unfortunately diminishing fast, vast swathes of rainforest remain untouched and unknown. Medium-sized creatures unknown to science continue to walk out of the Vietnamese canopy and no doubt other large interesting creatures still await discovery.

The notion that we are the only life in this fair universe of ours is laughable in the extreme. The mathematics dictate that there are more than enough planets out there similar to our own that could sustain life in some form or another. It may be that on some far away planet there exists a creature large enough to have King Kong for starters and Godzilla for the main course, using *T. rex* as a tooth pick afterwards. Yet animals do not need to be large to be deadly. Venomous creatures are testament enough to that. There exist life-forms that are far smaller than even insects and can prove far more deadly. Bacterial life-forms can prove deadly to even the largest, nastiest animal. We have developed many drugs to kill these internal invaders, but they are so progressive and adaptive that they can become resistant to our attacks remarkably quickly. So who is the Daddy; a 70-foot megalodon or viral bacteria so small that the naked eye cannot see it? That, ultimately, is for you the reader to decide....

THE CENTRE FOR FORTEAN ZOOLOGY

So, what is the Centre for Fortean Zoology?

We are a non profit-making organisation founded in 1992 with the aim of being a clearing house for information, and coordinating research into mystery animals around the world. We also study out of place animals, rare and aberrant animal behaviour, and Zooform Phenomena; little-understood "things" that appear to be animals, but which are in fact nothing of the sort, and not even alive (at least in the way we understand the term).

Why should I join the Centre for Fortean Zoology?

Not only are we the biggest organisation of our type in the world, but - or so we like to think - we are the best. We are certainly the only truly global Cryptozoological research organisation, and we carry out our investigations using a strictly scientific set of guidelines. We are expanding all the time and looking to recruit new members to help us in our research into mysterious animals and strange creatures across the globe. Why should you join us? Because, if you are genuinely interested in trying to solve the last great mysteries of Mother Nature, there is nobody better than us with whom to do it.

What do I get if I join the Centre for Fortean Zoology?

For £12 a year, you get a four-issue subscription to our journal *Animals & Men*. Each issue contains 60 pages packed with news, articles, letters, research papers, field reports, and even a gossip column! The magazine is A5 in format with a full colour cover. You also have access to one of the world's largest collections of resource material dealing with cryptozoology and allied disciplines, and people from the CFZ membership regularly take part in fieldwork and expeditions around the world.

How is the Centre for Fortean Zoology organized?

The CFZ is managed by a three-man board of trustees, with a non-profit making trust registered with HM Government Stamp Office. The board of trustees is supported by a Permanent Directorate of full and part-time staff, and advised by a Consultancy Board of specialists - many of whom are world-renowned experts in their particular field. We have regional representatives across the UK, the USA, and many other parts of the world, and are affiliated with other organisations whose aims and protocols mirror our own.

I am new to the subject, and although I am interested I have little practical knowledge. I don't want to feel out of my depth. What should I do?

Don't worry. We were *all* beginners once. You'll find that the people at the CFZ are friendly and approachable. We have a thriving forum on the website which is the hub of an ever-growing electronic community. You will soon find your feet. Many members of the CFZ Permanent Directorate started off as ordinary members, and now work full-time chasing monsters around the world.

I have an idea for a project which isn't on your website. What do I do?

Write to us, e-mail us, or telephone us. The list of future projects on the website is not exhaustive. If you have a good idea for an investigation, please tell us. We may well be able to help.

How do I go on an expedition?

We are always looking for volunteers to join us. If you see a project that interests you, do not hesitate to get in touch with us. Under certain circumstances we can help provide funding for your trip. If you look on the future projects section of the website, you can see some of the projects that we have pencilled in for the next few years.

In 2003 and 2004 we sent three-man expeditions to Sumatra looking for Orang-Pendek - a semi-legendary bipedal ape. The same three went to Mongolia in 2005. All three members started off merely subscribers to the CFZ magazine.

Next time it could be you!

Project Kerinci, Sumatra - 2003
In search of the bipedal ape Orang Pendek

How is the Centre for Fortean Zoology funded?

We have no magic sources of income. All our funds come from donations, membership fees, works that we do for TV, radio or magazines, and sales of our publications and merchandise. We are always looking for corporate sponsorship, and other sources of revenue. If you have any ideas for fund-raising please let us know. However, unlike other cryptozoological organisations in the past, we do not live in an intellectual ivory tower. We are not afraid to get our hands dirty, and furthermore we are not one of those organisations where the membership have to raise money so that a privileged few can go on expensive foreign trips. Our research teams, both in the UK and abroad, consist of a mixture of experienced and inexperienced personnel. We are truly a community, and work on the premise that the benefits of CFZ membership are open to all.

What do you do with the data you gather from your investigations and expeditions?

Reports of our investigations are published on our website as soon as they are available. Preliminary reports are posted within days of the project finishing.

Each year we publish a 200 page yearbook containing research papers and expedition reports too long to be printed in the journal. We freely circulate our information to anybody who asks for it.

Is the CFZ community purely an electronic one?

No. Each year since 2000 we have held our annual convention - the *Weird Weekend* - in Exeter. It is three days of lectures, workshops, and excursions. But most importantly it is a chance for members of the CFZ to meet each other, and to talk with the members of the permanent directorate in a relaxed and informal setting and preferably with a pint of beer in one hand. Since 2006 - the *Weird Weekend* has been bigger and better and held on the third weekend in August in the idyllic rural location of Woolsery in North Devon.

Since relocating to North Devon in 2005 we have become ever more closely involved with other community organisations, and we hope that this trend will continue. We also work closely with Police Forces across the UK as consultants for animal mutilation cases, and we intend to forge closer links with the coastguard and other community services. We want to work closely with those who regularly travel into the Bristol Channel, so that if the recent trend of exotic animal visitors to our coastal waters continues, we can be out there as soon as possible.

We are building a Visitor's Centre in rural North Devon. This will not be open to the general public, but will provide a museum, a library and an educational resource for our members (currently over 400) across the globe. We are also planning a youth organisation which will involve children and young people in our activities.

Apart from having been the only Fortean Zoological organisation in the world to have consistently published material on all aspects of the subject for over a decade, we have achieved the following concrete results:

- Disproved the myth relating to the headless so-called sea-serpent carcass of Durgan beach in Cornwall 1975
- Disproved the story of the 1988 puma skull of Lustleigh Cleave
- Carried out the only in-depth research ever into the mythos of the Cornish Owlman
- Made the first records of a tropical species of lamprey
- Made the first records of a luminous cave gnat larva in Thailand
- Discovered a possible new species of British mammal - the beech marten
- In 1994-6 carried out the first archival fortean zoological survey of Hong Kong
- In the year 2000, CFZ theories were confirmed when an new species of lizard was added to the British list
- Identified the monster of Martin Mere in Lancashire as a giant wels catfish
- Expanded the known range of Armitage's skink in the Gambia by 80%
- Obtained photographic evidence of the remains of Europe's largest known pike
- Carried out the first ever in-depth study of the *ninki-nanka*
- Carried out the first attempt to breed Puerto Rican cave snails in captivity
- Were the first European explorers to visit the `lost valley` in Sumatra
- Published the first ever evidence for a new tribe of pygmies in Guyana
- Published the first evidence for a new species of caiman in Guyana
- Filmed unknown creatures on a monster-haunted lake in Ireland for the first time
- Had a sighting of orang pendek in Sumatra in 2009
- Published some of the best evidence ever for the almasty in southern Russia

EXPEDITIONS & INVESTIGATIONS TO DATE INCLUDE:

- 1998 Puerto Rico, Florida, Mexico *(Chupacabras)*
- 1999 Nevada *(Bigfoot)*
- 2000 Thailand *(Giant snakes called nagas)*
- 2002 Martin Mere *(Giant catfish)*
- 2002 Cleveland *(Wallaby mutilation)*
- 2003 Bolam Lake *(BHM Reports)*
- 2003 Sumatra *(Orang Pendek)*
- 2003 Texas *(Bigfoot; giant snapping turtles)*
- 2004 Sumatra *(Orang Pendek; cigau, a sabre-toothed cat)*
- 2004 Illinois *(Black panthers; cicada swarm)*
- 2004 Texas *(Mystery blue dog)*
- Loch Morar *(Monster)*
- 2004 Puerto Rico *(Chupacabras; carnivorous cave snails)*
- 2005 Belize *(Affiliate expedition for hairy dwarfs)*
- 2005 Loch Ness *(Monster)*
- 2005 Mongolia *(Allghoi Khorkhoi aka Mongolian death worm)*
- 2006 Gambia *(Gambo - Gambian sea monster, Ninki Nanka and Armitage's skink*
- 2006 Llangorse Lake *(Giant pike, giant eels)*
- 2006 Windermere *(Giant eels)*
- 2007 Coniston Water *(Giant eels)*
- 2007 Guyana *(Giant anaconda, didi, water tiger)*
- 2008 Russia *(Almasty)*
- 2009 Sumatra *(Orang pendek)*
- 2009 Republic of Ireland *(Lake Monster)*

Other books available from
CFZ PRESS

CFZ PRESS

THE OWLMAN AND OTHERS - 30th Anniversary Edition
Jonathan Downes - ISBN 978-1-905723-02-7

£14.99

EASTER 1976 - Two young girls playing in the churchyard of Mawnan Old Church in southern Cornwall were frightened by what they described as a "nasty bird-man". A series of sightings that has continued to the present day. These grotesque and frightening episodes have fascinated researchers for three decades now, and one man has spent years collecting all the available evidence into a book. To mark the 30th anniversary of these sightings, Jonathan Downes has published a special edition of his book.

DRAGONS - More than a myth?
Richard Freeman - ISBN 0-9512872-9-X

£14.99

First scientific look at dragons since 1884. It looks at dragon legends worldwide, and examines modern sightings of dragon-like creatures, as well as some of the more esoteric theories surrounding dragonkind.

Dragons are discussed from a folkloric, historical and cryptozoological perspective, and Richard Freeman concludes that: "When your parents told you that dragons don't exist - they lied!"

MONSTER HUNTER
Jonathan Downes - ISBN 0-9512872-7-3

£14.99

Jonathan Downes' long-awaited autobiography, *Monster Hunter*...

Written with refreshing candour, it is the extraordinary story of an extraordinary life, in which the author crosses paths with wizards, rock stars, terrorists, and a bewildering array of mythical and not so mythical monsters, and still just about manages to emerge with his sanity intact........

MONSTER OF THE MERE
Jonathan Downes - ISBN 0-9512872-2-2

£12.50

It all starts on Valentine's Day 2002 when a Lancashire newspaper announces that "Something" has been attacking swans at a nature reserve in Lancashire. Eyewitnesses have reported that a giant unknown creature has been dragging fully grown swans beneath the water at Martin Mere. An intrepid team from the Exeter based Centre for Fortean Zoology, led by the author, make two trips – each of a week – to the lake and its surrounding marshlands. During their investigations they uncover a thrilling and complex web of historical fact and fancy, quasi Fortean occurrences, strange animals and even human sacrifice.

**CFZ PRESS, MYRTLE COTTAGE,
WOOLFARDISWORTHY BIDEFORD,
NORTH DEVON, EX39 5QR
www.cfz.org.uk**

Other books available from
CFZ PRESS

ONLY FOOLS AND GOATSUCKERS
Jonathan Downes - ISBN 0-9512872-3-0

£12.50

In January and February 1998 Jonathan Downes and Graham Inglis of the Centre for Fortean Zoology spent three and a half weeks in Puerto Rico, Mexico and Florida, accompanied by a film crew from UK Channel 4 TV. Their aim was to make a documentary about the terrifying chupacabra - a vampiric creature that exists somewhere in the grey area between folklore and reality. This remarkable book tells the gripping, sometimes scary, and often hilariously funny story of how the boys from the CFZ did their best to subvert the medium of contemporary TV documentary making and actually do their job.

WHILE THE CAT'S AWAY
Chris Moiser - ISBN: 0-9512872-1-4

£7.99

Over the past thirty years or so there have been numerous sightings of large exotic cats, including black leopards, pumas and lynx, in the South West of England. Former Rhodesian soldier Sam McCall moved to North Devon and became a farmer and pub owner when Rhodesia became Zimbabwe in 1980. Over the years despite many of his pub regulars having seen the "Beast of Exmoor" Sam wasn't at all sure that it existed. Then a series of happenings made him change his mind. Chris Moiser—a zoologist—is well known for his research into the mystery cats of the westcountry. This is his first novel.

CFZ EXPEDITION REPORT 2006 - GAMBIA
ISBN 1905723032

£12.50

In July 2006, The J.T.Downes memorial Gambia Expedition - a six-person team - Chris Moiser, Richard Freeman, Chris Clarke, Oll Lewis, Lisa Dowley and Suzi Marsh went to the Gambia, West Africa. They went in search of a dragon-like creature, known to the natives as `Ninki Nanka`, which has terrorized the tiny African state for generations, and has reportedly killed people as recently as the 1990s. They also went to dig up part of a beach where an amateur naturalist claims to have buried the carcass of a mysterious fifteen foot sea monster named 'Gambo', and they sought to find the Armitage's Skink (*Chalcides armitagei*) - a tiny lizard first described in 1922 and only rediscovered in 1989. Here, for the first time, is their story.... With an forward by Dr. Karl Shuker and introduction by Jonathan Downes.

BIG CATS IN BRITAIN YEARBOOK 2006
Edited by Mark Fraser - ISBN 978-1905723-01-0

£10.00

Big cats are said to roam the British Isles and Ireland even now as you are sitting and reading this. People from all walks of life encounter these mysterious felines on a daily basis in every nook and cranny of these two countries. Most are jet-black, some are white, some are brown, in fact big cats of every description and colour are seen by some unsuspecting person while on his or her daily business. 'Big Cats in Britain' are the largest and most active group in the British Isles and Ireland This is their first book. It contains a run-down of every known big cat sighting in the UK during 2005, together with essays by various luminaries of the British big cat research community which place the phenomenon into scientific, cultural, and historical perspective.

CFZ PRESS, MYRTLE COTTAGE, WOOLSERY, BIDEFORD, NORTH DEVON, EX39 5QR
www.cfz.org.uk

Other books available from
CFZ PRESS

THE SMALLER MYSTERY CARNIVORES OF THE WESTCOUNTRY
Jonathan Downes - **ISBN** 978-1-905723-05-8

£7.99

Although much has been written in recent years about the mystery big cats which have been reported stalking Westcountry moorlands, little has been written on the subject of the smaller British mystery carnivores. This unique book redresses the balance and examines the current status in the Westcountry of three species thought to be extinct: the Wildcat, the Pine Marten and the Polecat, finding that the truth is far more exciting than the currently held scientific dogma. This book also uncovers evidence suggesting that even more exotic species of small mammal may lurk hitherto unsuspected in the countryside of Devon, Cornwall, Somerset and Dorset.

THE BLACKDOWN MYSTERY
Jonathan Downes - **ISBN** 978-1-905723-00-3

£7.99

Intrepid members of the CFZ are up to the challenge, and manage to entangle themselves thoroughly in the bizarre trappings of this case. This is the soft underbelly of ufology, rife with unsavoury characters, plenty of drugs and booze." That sums it up quite well, we think. A new edition of the classic 1999 book by legendary fortean author Jonathan Downes. In this remarkable book, Jon weaves a complex tale of conspiracy, anti-conspiracy, quasi-conspiracy and downright lies surrounding an air-crash and alleged UFO incident in Somerset during 1996. However the story is much stranger than that. This excellent and amusing book lifts the lid off much of contemporary forteana and explains far more than it initially promises.

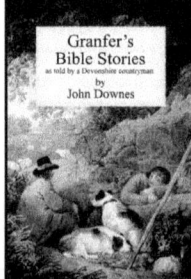

GRANFER'S BIBLE STORIES
John Downes - **ISBN** 0-9512872-8-1

£7.99

Bible stories in the Devonshire vernacular, each story being told by an old Devon Grandfather - 'Granfer'. These stories are now collected together in a remarkable book presenting selected parts of the Bible as one more-or-less continuous tale in short 'bite sized' stories intended for dipping into or even for bed-time reading. `Granfer` treats the biblical characters as if they were simple country folk living in the next village. Many of the stories are treated with a degree of bucolic humour and kindly irreverence, which not only gives the reader an opportunity to re-evaluate familiar tales in a new light, but do so in both an entertaining and a spiritually uplifting manner.

FRAGRANT HARBOURS DISTANT RIVERS
John Downes - **ISBN** 0-9512872-5-7

£12.50

Many excellent books have been written about Africa during the second half of the 19th Century, but this one is unique in that it presents the stories of a dozen different people, whose interlinked lives and achievements have as many nuances as any contemporary soap opera. It explains how the events in China and Hong Kong which surrounded the Opium Wars, intimately effected the events in Africa which take up the majority of this book. The author served in the Colonial Service in Nigeria and Hong Kong, during which he found himself following in the footsteps of one of the main characters in this book; Frederick Lugard – the architect of modern Nigeria.

**CFZ PRESS, MYRTLE COTTAGE,
WOOLFARDISWORTHY BIDEFORD,
NORTH DEVON, EX39 5QR
w w w . c f z . o r g . u k**

Other books available from
CFZ PRESS

ANIMALS & MEN - Issues 1 - 5 - In the Beginning
Edited by Jonathan Downes - ISBN 0-9512872-6-5

£12.50

At the beginning of the 21st Century monsters still roam the remote, and sometimes not so remote, corners of our planet. It is our job to search for them. The Centre for Fortean Zoology [CFZ] is the only professional, scientific and full-time organisation in the world dedicated to cryptozoology - the study of unknown animals. Since 1992 the CFZ has carried out an unparalleled programme of research and investigation all over the world. We have carried out expeditions to Sumatra (2003 and 2004), Mongolia (2005), Puerto Rico (1998 and 2004), Mexico (1998), Thailand (2000), Florida (1998), Nevada (1999 and 2003), Texas (2003 and 2004), and Illinois (2004). An introductory essay by Jonathan Downes, notes putting each issue into a historical perspective, and a history of the CFZ.

ANIMALS & MEN - Issues 6 - 10 - The Number of the Beast
Edited by Jonathan Downes - ISBN 978-1-905723-06-5

£12.50

At the beginning of the 21st Century monsters still roam the remote, and sometimes not so remote, corners of our planet. It is our job to search for them. The Centre for Fortean Zoology [CFZ] is the only professional, scientific and full-time organisation in the world dedicated to cryptozoology - the study of unknown animals. Since 1992 the CFZ has carried out an unparalleled programme of research and investigation all over the world. We have carried out expeditions to Sumatra (2003 and 2004), Mongolia (2005), Puerto Rico (1998 and 2004), Mexico (1998), Thailand (2000), Florida (1998), Nevada (1999 and 2003), Texas (2003 and 2004), and Illinois (2004). Preface by Mark North and an introductory essay by Jonathan Downes, notes putting each issue into a historical perspective, and a history of the CFZ.

BIG BIRD! Modern Sightings of Flying Monsters
Ken Gerhard - ISBN 978-1-905723-08-9

£7.99

From all over the dusty U.S./Mexican border come hair-raising stories of modern day encounters with winged monsters of immense size and terrifying appearance. Further field sightings of similar creatures are recorded from all around the globe. What lies behind these weird tales? Ken Gerhard is a native Texan, he lives in the homeland of the monster some call 'Big Bird'. Ken's scholarly work is the first of its kind. On the track of the monster, Ken uncovers cases of animal mutilations, attacks on humans and mounting evidence of a stunning zoological discovery ignored by mainstream science. Keep watching the skies!

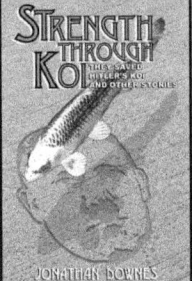

STRENGTH THROUGH KOI
They saved Hitler's Koi and other stories

£7.99

Jonathan Downes - **ISBN** 978-1-905723-04-1

Strength through Koi is a book of short stories - some of them true, some of them less so - by noted cryptozoologist and raconteur Jonathan Downes. The stories are all about koi carp, and their interaction with bigfoot, UFOs, and Nazis. Even the late George Harrison makes an appearance. Very funny in parts, this book is highly recommended for anyone with even a passing interest in aquaculture, but should be taken definitely *cum grano salis*.

CFZ PRESS, MYRTLE COTTAGE, WOOLSERY, BIDEFORD, NORTH DEVON, EX39 5QR

Other books available from
CFZ PRESS

BIG CATS IN BRITAIN YEARBOOK 2007
Edited by Mark Fraser - ISBN 978-1-905723-09-6

£12.50

People from all walks of life encounter mysterious felids on a daily basis, in every nook and cranny of the UK. Most are jet-black, some are white, some are brown; big cats of every description and colour are seen by some unsuspecting person while on his or her daily business. 'Big Cats in Britain' are the largest and most active research group in the British Isles and Ireland. This book contains a run-down of every known big cat sighting in the UK during 2006, together with essays by various luminaries of the British big cat research community.

CAT FLAPS! Northern Mystery Cats
Andy Roberts - ISBN 978-1-905723-11-9

£6.99

Of all Britain's mystery beasts, the alien big cats are the most renowned. In recent years the notoriety of these uncatchable, out-of-place predators have eclipsed even the Loch Ness Monster. They slink from the shadows to terrorise a community, and then, as often as not, vanish like ghosts. But now film, photographs, livestock kills, and paw prints show that we can no longer deny the existence of these once-legendary beasts. Here then is a case-study, a true lost classic of Fortean research by one of the country's most respected researchers.

CENTRE FOR FORTEAN ZOOLOGY 2007 YEARBOOK
Edited by Jonathan Downes and Richard Freeman
ISBN 978-1-905723-14-0

£12.50

The Centre For Fortean Zoology Yearbook is a collection of papers and essays too long and detailed for publication in the CFZ Journal *Animals & Men*. With contributions from both well-known researchers, and relative newcomers to the field, the Yearbook provides a forum where new theories can be expounded, and work on little-known cryptids discussed.

MONSTER! THE A-Z OF ZOOFORM PHENOMENA
Neil Arnold - ISBN 978-1-905723-10-2

£14.99

Zooform Phenomena are the most elusive, and least understood, mystery `animals`. Indeed, they are not animals at all, and are not even animate in the accepted terms of the word. Author and researcher Neil Arnold is to be commended for a groundbreaking piece of work, and has provided the world's first alphabetical listing of zooforms from around the world.

**CFZ PRESS, MYRTLE COTTAGE,
WOOLFARDISWORTHY BIDEFORD,
NORTH DEVON, EX39 5QR
www.cfz.org.uk**

Other books available from
CFZ PRESS

BIG CATS LOOSE IN BRITAIN
Marcus Matthews - ISBN 978-1-905723-12-6

£14.99

Big Cats: Loose in Britain, looks at the body of anecdotal evidence for such creatures: sightings, livestock kills, paw-prints and photographs, and seeks to determine underlying commonalities and threads of evidence. These two strands are repeatedly woven together into a highly readable, yet scientifically compelling, overview of the big cat phenomenon in Britain.

DARK DORSET
TALES OF MYSTERY, WONDER AND TERROR
Robert. J. Newland and Mark. J. North
ISBN 978-1-905723-15-6

£12.50

This extensively illustrated compendium has over 400 tales and references, making this book by far one of the best in its field. Dark Dorset has been thoroughly researched, and includes many new entries and up to date information never before published. The title of the book speaks for itself, and is indeed not for the faint hearted or those easily shocked.

MAN-MONKEY - IN SEARCH OF THE BRITISH BIGFOOT
Nick Redfern - ISBN 978-1-905723-16-4

£9.99

In her 1883 book, *Shropshire Folklore*, Charlotte S. Burne wrote: *'Just before he reached the canal bridge, a strange black creature with great white eyes sprang out of the plantation by the roadside and alighted on his horse's back'*. The creature duly became known as the `Man-Monkey`.

Between 1986 and early 2001, Nick Redfern delved deeply into the mystery of the strange creature of that dark stretch of canal. Now, published for the very first time, are Nick's original interview notes, his files and discoveries; as well as his theories pertaining to what lies at the heart of this diabolical legend.

EXTRAORDINARY ANIMALS REVISITED
Dr Karl Shuker - ISBN 978-1905723171

£14.99

This delightful book is the long-awaited, greatly-expanded new edition of one of Dr Karl Shuker's much-loved early volumes, *Extraordinary Animals Worldwide*. It is a fascinating celebration of what used to be called romantic natural history, examining a dazzling diversity of animal anomalies, creatures of cryptozoology, and all manner of other thought-provoking zoological revelations and continuing controversies down through the ages of wildlife discovery.

**CFZ PRESS, MYRTLE COTTAGE,
WOOLFARDISWORTHY BIDEFORD,
NORTH DEVON, EX39 5QR
w w w . c f z . o r g . u k**

Other books available from
CFZ PRESS

DARK DORSET CALENDAR CUSTOMS
Robert J Newland - ISBN 978-1-905723-18-8

£12.50

Much of the intrinsic charm of Dorset folklore is owed to the importance of folk customs. Today only a small amount of these curious and occasionally eccentric customs have survived, while those that still continue have, for many of us, lost their original significance. Why do we eat pancakes on Shrove Tuesday? Why do children dance around the maypole on May Day? Why do we carve pumpkin lanterns at Hallowe'en? All the answers are here! Robert has made an in-depth study of the Dorset country calendar identifying the major feast-days, holidays and celebrations when traditionally such folk customs are practiced.

CENTRE FOR FORTEAN ZOOLOGY 2004 YEARBOOK
Edited by Jonathan Downes and Richard Freeman
ISBN 978-1-905723-14-0

£12.50

The Centre For Fortean Zoology Yearbook is a collection of papers and essays too long and detailed for publication in the CFZ Journal *Animals & Men*. With contributions from both well-known researchers, and relative newcomers to the field, the Yearbook provides a forum where new theories can be expounded, and work on little-known cryptids discussed.

CENTRE FOR FORTEAN ZOOLOGY 2008 YEARBOOK
Edited by Jonathan Downes and Corinna Downes
ISBN 978-1-905723-19-5

£12.50

The Centre For Fortean Zoology Yearbook is a collection of papers and essays too long and detailed for publication in the CFZ Journal *Animals & Men*. With contributions from both well-known researchers, and relative newcomers to the field, the Yearbook provides a forum where new theories can be expounded, and work on little-known cryptids discussed.

ETHNA'S JOURNAL
Corinna Newton Downes
ISBN 978-1-905723-21-8

£9.99

Ethna's Journal tells the story of a few months in an alternate Dark Ages, seen through the eyes of Ethna, daughter of Lord Edric. She is an unsophisticated girl from the fortress town of Cragnuth, somewhere in the north of England, who reluctantly gets embroiled in a web of treachery, sorcery and bloody war...

**CFZ PRESS, MYRTLE COTTAGE,
WOOLFARDISWORTHY BIDEFORD,
NORTH DEVON, EX39 5QR
www.cfz.org.uk**

Other books available from
CFZ PRESS

ANIMALS & MEN - Issues 11 - 15 - The Call of the Wild
Jonathan Downes (Ed) - ISBN 978-1-905723-07-2

£12.50

Since 1994 we have been publishing the world's only dedicated cryptozoology magazine, *Animals & Men*. This volume contains fascimile reprints of issues 11 to 15 and includes articles covering out of place walruses, feathered dinosaurs, possible North American ground sloth survival, the theory of initial bipedalism, mystery whales, mitten crabs in Britain, Barbary lions, out of place animals in Germany, mystery pangolins, the barking beast of Bath, Yorkshire ABCs, Molly the singing oyster, singing mice, the dragons of Yorkshire, singing mice, the bigfoot murders, waspman, British beavers, the migo, Nessie, the weird warbling whatsit of the westcountry, the quagga project and much more...

IN THE WAKE OF BERNARD HEUVELMANS
Michael A Woodley - ISBN 978-1-905723-20-1

£9.99

Everyone is familiar with the nautical maps from the middle ages that were liberally festooned with images of exotic and monstrous animals, but the truth of the matter is that the *idea* of the sea monster is probably as old as humankind itself.

For two hundred years, scientists have been producing speculative classifications of sea serpents, attempting to place them within a zoological framework. This book looks at these successive classification models, and using a new formula produces a sea serpent classification for the 21st Century.

CENTRE FOR FORTEAN ZOOLOGY 1999 YEARBOOK
Edited by Jonathan Downes
ISBN 978 -1-905723-24-9

£12.50

The Centre For Fortean Zoology Yearbook is a collection of papers and essays too long and detailed for publication in the CFZ Journal *Animals & Men*. With contributions from both well-known researchers, and relative newcomers to the field, the Yearbook provides a forum where new theories can be expounded, and work on little-known cryptids discussed.

CENTRE FOR FORTEAN ZOOLOGY 1996 YEARBOOK
Edited by Jonathan Downes
ISBN 978 -1-905723-22-5

£12.50

The Centre For Fortean Zoology Yearbook is a collection of papers and essays too long and detailed for publication in the CFZ Journal *Animals & Men*. With contributions from both well-known researchers, and relative newcomers to the field, the Yearbook provides a forum where new theories can be expounded, and work on little-known cryptids discussed.

**CFZ PRESS, MYRTLE COTTAGE,
WOOLFARDISWORTHY BIDEFORD,
NORTH DEVON, EX39 5QR
www.cfz.org.uk**

Other books available from
CFZ PRESS

BIG CATS IN BRITAIN YEARBOOK 2008
Edited by Mark Fraser - ISBN 978-1-905723-23-2

£12.50

People from all walks of life encounter mysterious felids on a daily basis, in every nook and cranny of the UK. Most are jet-black, some are white, some are brown; big cats of every description and colour are seen by some unsuspecting person while on his or her daily business. 'Big Cats in Britain' are the largest and most active research group in the British Isles and Ireland. This book contains a run-down of every known big cat sighting in the UK during 2007, together with essays by various luminaries of the British big cat research community.

CFZ EXPEDITION REPORT 2007 - GUYANA
ISBN 978-1-905723-25-6

£12.50

Since 1992, the CFZ has carried out an unparalleled programme of research and investigation all over the world. In November 2007, a five-person team - Richard Freeman, Chris Clarke, Paul Rose, Lisa Dowley and Jon Hare went to Guyana, South America. They went in search of giant anacondas, the bigfoot-like didi, and the terrifying water tiger.

Here, for the first time, is their story...With an introduction by Jonathan Downes and forward by Dr. Karl Shuker.

CENTRE FOR FORTEAN ZOOLOGY 2003 YEARBOOK
Edited by Jonathan Downes and Richard Freeman
ISBN 978 -1-905723-19-5

£12.50

The Centre For Fortean Zoology Yearbook is a collection of papers and essays too long and detailed for publication in the CFZ Journal *Animals & Men*. With contributions from both well-known researchers, and relative newcomers to the field, the Yearbook provides a forum where new theories can be expounded, and work on little-known cryptids discussed.

CENTRE FOR FORTEAN ZOOLOGY 1997 YEARBOOK
Edited by Jonathan Downes and Graham Inglis
ISBN 978 -1-905723-27-0

£12.50

The Centre For Fortean Zoology Yearbook is a collection of papers and essays too long and detailed for publication in the CFZ Journal *Animals & Men*. With contributions from both well-known researchers, and relative newcomers to the field, the Yearbook provides a forum where new theories can be expounded, and work on little-known cryptids discussed.

**CFZ PRESS, MYRTLE COTTAGE,
WOOLFARDISWORTHY BIDEFORD,
NORTH DEVON, EX39 5QR
w w w . c f z . o r g . u k**

Other books available from
CFZ PRESS

CENTRE FOR FORTEAN ZOOLOGY 2000-1 YEARBOOK
Edited by Jonathan Downes and Richard Freeman
ISBN 978-1-905723-19-5

£12.50

The Centre For Fortean Zoology Yearbook is a collection of papers and essays too long and detailed for publication in the CFZ Journal *Animals & Men*. With contributions from both well-known researchers, and relative newcomers to the field, the Yearbook provides a forum where new theories can be expounded, and work on little-known cryptids discussed.

THE MYSTERY ANIMALS OF THE BRITISH ISLES: NORTHUMBERLAND AND TYNESIDE
Michael J Hallowell
ISBN 978-1-905723-29-4

£12.50

Mystery animals? Great Britain? Surely not. But is is true.

This is a major new series from CFZ Press. It will cover Great Britain and the Republic of Ireland, on a county by county basis, describing the mystery animals of the entire island group.

The Island of Paradise: Chupacabra, UFO Crash Retrievals, and Accelerated Evolution on the Island of Puerto Rico
Jonathan Downes - ISBN 978-1-905723-32-4

£14.99

In his first book of original research for four years, Jon Downes visits the Antillean island of Puerto Rico, to which he has led two expeditions - in 1998 and 2004. Together with noted researcher Nick Redfern he goes in search of the grotesque vampiric chupacabra, believing that it can - finally - be categorised within a zoological frame of reference rather than a purely paranormal one. Along the way he uncovers mystery after mystery, has a run in with terrorists, art historians, and even has his garden buzzed by a UFO. By turns both terrifying and funny, this remarkable book is a real tour de force by one of the world's foremost cryptozoological researchers.

DR SHUKER'S CASEBOOK
Dr Karl Shuker - ISBN 978-1905723-33-1

£14.99

Although he is best-known for his extensive cryptozoological researches and publications, Dr Karl Shuker has also investigated a very diverse range of other anomalies and unexplained phenomena, both in the literature and in the field. Now, compiled here for the very first time, are some of the extraordinary cases that he has re-examined or personally explored down through the years.

**CFZ PRESS, MYRTLE COTTAGE,
WOOLFARDISWORTHY BIDEFORD,
NORTH DEVON, EX39 5QR
www.cfz.org.uk**

Other books available from
CFZ PRESS

Dinosaurs and Other Prehistoric Animals on Stamps: A Worldwide Catalogue
Dr Karl P.N.Shuker - ISBN 978-1-905723-34-8

£9.99

Compiled by zoologist Dr Karl P.N. Shuker, a lifelong, enthusiastic collector of wildlife stamps and with an especial interest in those that portray fossil species, it provides an exhaustive, definitive listing of stamps and miniature sheets depicting dinosaurs and other prehistoric animals issued by countries throughout the world. It also includes sections dealing with cryptozoological stamps, dinosaur stamp superlatives, and unofficial prehistoric animal stamps.

CFZ EXPEDITION REPORT 2008 - RUSSIA
ISBN 978-1-905723-35-5

Since 1992, the CFZ has carried out an unparalleled programme of research and investigation all over the world. In July 2008, a five-person team - Richard Freeman, Chris Clarke, Dave Archer, Adam Davies and Keith Townley went to Kabardino-Balkaria in southern Russia in search of the almasty, maybe mankind's closest relative. Here, for the first time, is their story...With an introduction by Jonathan Downes and forward by Dr. Karl Shuker.

CENTRE FOR FORTEAN ZOOLOGY 2009 YEARBOOK
Edited by Jonathan Downes and Richard Freeman
ISBN 978 -1-905723-37

£12.50

The Centre For Fortean Zoology Yearbook is a collection of papers and essays too long and detailed for publication in the CFZ Journal *Animals & Men*. With contributions from both well-known researchers, and relative newcomers to the field, the Yearbook provides a forum where new theories can be expounded, and work on little-known cryptids discussed.

THE MYSTERY ANIMALS OF THE BRITISH ISLES: KENT
Neil Arnold
ISBN 978-1-905723-36-2

£12.50

Mystery animals? Great Britain? Surely not. But is is true.

This is a major new series from CFZ Press. It will cover Great Britain and the Republic of Ireland, on a county by county basis, describing the mystery animals of the entire island group.

**CFZ PRESS, MYRTLE COTTAGE,
WOOLFARDISWORTHY BIDEFORD,
NORTH DEVON, EX39 5QR
w w w . c f z . o r g . u k**

Other books available from
CFZ PRESS

GIANT SNAKES
By Michael Newton
ISBN: 978-1-905723-39-3

£9.99

In this exciting book, Michael Newton takes an overview of the most terrifying uberpredators in the world - giant snakes. Outsized examples of known species as well as putative new species are looked at in detail.

THE MYSTERY ANIMALS OF THE BRITISH ISLES:
THE WESTERN ISLES
Glen Vaudrey
ISBN 978-1-905723-42-3

£12.50

Mystery animals? Great Britain? Surely not. But is is true.

This is a major new series from CFZ Press. It will cover Great Britain and the Republic of Ireland, on a county by county basis, describing the mystery animals of the entire island group.

Strangely Strange but Oddly Normal
Andy Roberts
ISBN 978-1-905723-44-7

£14.99

An anthology of writings from one of Britain's most respected Fortean authors, covering everything from UFOs, to the Rolling Stones, and from psychedelic drugs to ancient fertility symbols, the Incredible String Band, and government cover-ups.

China: The Yellow Peril?
Richard Muirhead
ISBN 978-1-905723-41-6

£7.99

Richard Muirhead takes an in depth look at the history of Western relationships with China. If some Victorian antiquarians are to be believed contact between the Chinese Empire and other Middle Eastern and Western Empires goes back to times long before the birth of Christ, such as the ancient Egyptians and the Roman Empire.

**CFZ PRESS, MYRTLE COTTAGE,
WOOLFARDISWORTHY BIDEFORD,
NORTH DEVON, EX39 5QR
www.cfz.org.uk**

Other books available from
CFZ PRESS

STAR STEEDS AND OTHER DREAMS
By Dr Karl Shuker
ISBN-13: 978-1905723409

£8.99

Today, Dr Karl Shuker is a world-renowned author on cryptozoology and animal mythology, with over a dozen books and countless articles to his name, but long before his first book on such subjects had been published he was already a prolific poet. Yet in stark contrast to his continuing output of scientific writings, his poetry has remained largely unseen by the outside world - only his family, friends, and selected colleagues have ever read any of his very sizeable collection of poems...until now.

PREDATOR DEATHMATCH
By Nick Molloy
ISBN: 978-1-905723-45-4

£8.99

Predator Deathmatch is the first ever book to study apex predators and actually pose the question of who is/was the ultimate predator by pitting them against each other. The author has carefully profiled each contender with a mixture of historical data, information from the fossil record and current observations of wild animal behaviour. .

**CFZ PRESS, MYRTLE COTTAGE,
WOOLFARDISWORTHY BIDEFORD,
NORTH DEVON, EX39 5QR
w w w . c f z . o r g . u k**